GARDENS
OF
EARTHLY
DELIGHT

Patricia
Corbin

✦

GARDENS
OF
EARTHLY
DELIGHT

✦

Designs for the Good Life

E. P. Dutton   New York

(*Front endpapers*) This seaside garden in Maine glows with windblown drifts of sparkling color.

(*Pages ii–iii*) The dazzling white *Cerastium tomentosum* (snow-in-summer) enlivens New England's gray, lichened rocks.

(*Back endpapers*) These bountiful summer blooms are part of the backyard paradise at The Red Crow antiques shop in Pound Ridge, New York.

First published, 1985, in the United States by E. P. Dutton, Inc., 2 Park Avenue, New York, N.Y. 10016. All rights reserved under International and Pan-American Copyright Conventions. No part of this publication may be reproduced or transmitted in any form or by any means, electronic or mechanical, including photocopy, recording or any information storage and retrieval system now known or to be invented, without permission in writing from the publisher, except by a reviewer who wishes to quote brief passages in connection with a review written for inclusion in a magazine, newspaper or broadcast. Library of Congress Catalog Card Number: 85-70223 ISBN: 0-525-24335-6 Published simultaneously in Canada by Fitzhenry & Whiteside Limited, Toronto. Printed and bound by Dai Nippon Printing Co., Ltd., Tokyo, Japan. W 10 9 8 7 6 5 4 3 2 1 First Edition

With special thanks to Lynden B. Miller and Jan Moss, who led the way
up and down garden paths; grateful thanks to Thomas H. Everett of
The New York Botanical Garden, who gave my manuscript the
benefit of his encyclopedic knowledge; and with deepest
thanks to all the great gardeners whose beautiful
places are pictured in this book.

It is a very good thing to keep a gardening notebook. One may only carry out a twentieth part of its commands, but even that twentieth part has its effect. If it were not for my gardening notebook I should never have planted those daffodils in the farther meadow, in a bold, brave line, like a golden sword slashing through the fields of spring. I should never have beribboned the banks of the brook with bluebells... and if you think that "beribboned" is an affected verb you are wrong, for that is just how the bluebells look when you stand away from them with the west wind blowing... flying streamers of colour fluttering in the long grass.

If it had not been for my gardening notebook I should have forgotten the scarlet oaks which blaze so fiercely in October that a man may warm his hands at them. And at the end of May, in the front garden, when the wall flowers have come up, and the baby snapdragons have gone in, there would have been no colour in the garden at all had my notebook not reminded me that down the centre walk I could have a mist of cat mint, and against the hedges a carnival of giant poppies, pale pink, rose, and scarlet... those superbly intoxicated flowers that are like Southern girls....

Beverley Nichols, *A Village in a Valley*

There's a Garden in Everyone and a Garden Can Be Anywhere at All

On a table in a vase

Or in a garden room

Or Almost Anywhere You Care to Look

Looking like an Impressionist painting, a field of columbines, coralbells, and irises leads to a gazebo filled with tuberous begonias.

A backyard garden overflowing with old-fashioned charms
in a profusion of colors and textures.

A waterside garden in Maine planted with a lavish hand, the blooms tumbling over one another in a flurry of color.

The Conservatory at Wave Hill, an extravagance of beauty unfolding at Christmas and filled with blooms throughout the year.

A Newport gardener's sturdy work boots, taking the air in front of his cottage and catching the last rays of the sun.

CONTENTS

Up and Down Garden Paths

My small garden perched on a natural outcropping in front of our cottage is a good example of happenstance planting (Gertrude Jekyll would not approve). However, the color scheme looks a little more subdued after the rampant pink roses go—then the white hostas follow, along with yellow coreopsis and blue browallia. (The variegated hostas at the bottom of the pile seeded themselves.) They are "volunteers," along with Queen Anne's lace, which blooms later in a lovely filmy disorder. I never knew (before doing this book) that a volunteer *is a surprise seedling; it can happen in a garden in the form of a tree, a perennial, even an annual that just suddenly springs up in the most mysterious (and happy) way.*

1

I've always dreamed of having a garden to gloat over, filled with a rush of rapturous color of blowsy blooms spilling over themselves in fragrant abandon (like wading through Monet's Giverny, chin-high in flowers). But what with one thing and another it has never happened for me out here on the edge of the Atlantic. Then too, 1984 was a very bad year: even in April there were blizzards, and in May and June we had torrential rains. It was a fierce bad winter and a fiercer spring, and gardeners everywhere were wringing their hands over the bad conditions.

Even with such terrible weather there were extra-ordinarily lovely gardens to photograph this past summer, ranging from Zones 7 through 3, from Maine down to the Main Line, showing June through September and even October blooms. The whole glorious summer was one continuous, joyous sightseeing tour of these special places, and I never had a better time, even with the hay fever problem and the bee stings.

In this book you will find wonderful surprises, pictures of whimsies and sculptures, of follies and flourishes; there are soft, romantic garden scenes to revel in as well as a lot of enchanting and practical design ideas to copy. They are glowing inspirations for all of us who haven't quite been able to manage the same effects at home. Time and effort have a lot to do with it: some of these gardens are over fifty years old, and not one of them is under five. Gardening *is* a passionate pursuit all through life. Vita Sackville-West said it best in her book *A Joy of Gardening,* "The more one gardens, the more one learns; and the more one learns, the more one realizes how little one knows. I suppose the whole of life is like that."

Well, yes, the learning goes on and this book is dedicated to

> All great gardeners everywhere
>   who see their own gardens as places that
>   change and develop as time goes by.

A great gardener always invites you to "come back again next year."

A LITTLE LATIN

It is remarkable how many plants that began life in Africa or China or the Himalayas can settle down in someone's backyard and grow happily ever after. In dictionaries and catalogues we can look up any plant and find out where it came from, what colors it comes in, its type of foliage, as well as its potential size and preference in soil and climate. Reading about *Achillea millefolium* (yarrow) from a catalogue we learn:

> **ACHILLEA** (ack-ill-lee-a) **Compositae.** Yarrow. This valuable garden plant from the north temperate zone is widely grown for the masses of flowers it bears throughout most of the summer. The foliage is attractive and fern-like. It grows well in dry, exposed places and is not fussy about soil, but does best in a good garden loam. May be propagated by division in spring or fall. Hardy in *Zones 3 to 9* except where noted.

The plant supposedly grew in churchyards as a reproach to the dead "Who need never have come there if they had taken their yarrow broth faithfully every day while living." Yarrow also comes in 'Fire King,' a deep red, and 'Cerise Queen,' a rosy shade, and the plants grow about 24 inches tall—*A. filipendulina* from the Caucasus grows taller, up to 60 inches, and has platelike heads of yellow flowers and deeply cut, aromatic foliage. All the foregoing information (and even more) is readily available, and gardeners can easily pick and choose their plants accordingly.

Modern plant classification began with Swedish botanist Carl von Linné, who used the sex organs of plants as a base for a revolutionary new system of classification. In his *Genera Plantarum* (1737) and *Species Plantarum* (1753) he suggested identifying plants by using two Latin-form words, the first that of the genus, and the two together designating the species. It was a brilliant, systematic method, and his own Latinized name, Carolus Linnaeus, became well known for this extraordinary achievement. He became renowned as the great man of Swedish natural science, with botanists all over the world revering his work.

Thanks to him, gardening encyclopedias list plants under genus and species along with descriptions.

Genus is the name given to a group of related plants. Thus all roses, whatever their names or their kinds, belong to the Rose genus and in botanical Latin all their names will begin with *Rosa*. Species are natural subdivisions recognized within a genus. Varieties, or cultivars, are natural or horticultural variants of species. In the case of perennial flax *(Linum perenne album)*, the genus name, *Linum,* is followed by *perenne* to define the species, and *album,* which indicates a white-flowered variety. In some genera and species there are at least two and sometimes dozens of varieties and hybrids. A hybrid is a cross between two species of the same, or less commonly of different, genera. A multiplication sign before the name of a plant means that the plant is a recognized hybrid. In plant language the first word of a name indicates the genus and the second the species. *Campanula,* for instance, comes from the Latin word for "bell" and its common name is bellflower. There are hundreds of species and varieties and using English to designate them would be cumbersome. That is why botanical names can help in selecting plants for their color, habits, description, and place of origin. For instance, *Artemisia lactiflora* has white flowers; *Morina longifolia* shows off exceptionally long leaves; *Campanula persicifolia is* peach-leaved; *Hordeum jubatum,* commonly called "squirreltail grass," is crested like a mane; and *Helipterum roseum* has rosy-pink blooms.

If a plant is a *"japonica,"* it probably comes from Japan; *"australis,"* from the Southern Hemisphere; or *"canadensis,"* from North America. *Rotundifolia* means "round-leaved," and *lunate* means "shaped like a crescent moon."

Some words describe growing habits: *reptans, repens,* and *procumbens* mean creeping; *divaricata* means spreading or growing in a straggling way. A plant can be *"gloriosus," "impressus," "superbus," "nocturnum," "amabilis,"* even *"obtusa," "obliqua"* or *"ambigua."*

The following are some descriptive words to look for in buying plants:

alba	white
argentea	silvery
azurea	blue
chrysantha	golden
cineraria	ash-colored
deliciosus	delicious
divaricata	spreading
flavum	yellow
flore-pleno	having double flowers
floribunda	flowering freely
foetida	ill-scented
fruticosa	shrubby
fulva	orange-red
glauca	gray-green or blue-green
gloriosa	glorious
gracilis	slender
grandiflora	large-flowered
graveolens	heavily-scented
incana	hoary-gray
jubatum	crested like a mane
lactiflora	with milk-white flowers
lanata	woolly
longifolia	long-leaved
lunata	shaped like a crescent moon
luteum	yellow
maxima	largest
microphyllus	small-leaved
millefolium	thousand-leaved
minor	small
nana	dwarf
niveum	snow-white
nobilis	celebrated and well-known
pendula	weeping
persicifolia	peach-leaved
plumosa	feathery
polyanthus	many-flowered
procumbens	creeping
purpurea	purple
repens	creeping
reptans	creeping
rotundifolia	round-leaved
rubra	red
senescens	gray
spectabilis	showy
velutinus	velvety
vulgaris	common and usual

I.
Creating Peaceable Kingdoms

NATURE'S HELP

Good garden help is hard to find, but when nature lends a hand, it supplies the best: bees and butterflies, ladybugs and dragonflies, and perhaps the biggest help of all, downright ugly toads. Some of these creatures eat other creatures that eat flowers and leaves. The other desirables, like bees and butterflies, fertilize and pollinate. Some of these good workers can be attracted; others can be purchased: every year a town in Maine buys about 12,000 dragonflies to battle its mosquito problem. The dragonflies do a double job destroying the mosquitoes: they eat the larvae first; then if there are any survivors, they catch them on the wing. (This help costs about $2,000, and is supplied by the Connecticut Valley Biological Supply Company in Southampton, Massachusetts.) Ladybugs can also be bought and let loose in the garden to chew aphids, mealybugs, spider mites, and whiteflies. (One pint of ladybugs, about 9,000 of them, costs $13.50, plus $3.95 for postage, from Lakeland Nurseries, Hanover, Pennsylvania 17331.)

For spreading blooms about, bees and butterflies are the nicest garden friends to have around. To attract them you have to know what they like best. The bees go for certain colors, and butterflies head for the sweetest scents. A mecca for bees is monarda (bee balm) and one for butterflies is buddleia.

Some gardeners believe that souls return to earth as butterflies. (The Aztecs did too.) To attract them Winston Churchill had a summerhouse at Chartwell turned into a butterfly haven where chrysalids could safely unfold to become winged creatures.

If you have yellow, blue, mauve, purple, and reddish-

Nature's help in spreading the blooms.

blue flowers blooming in drifts and clumps, you will have bees aplenty, all busy fertilizing and pollinating. Sweet attractions for butterflies and moths are flowers that smell very much like the insects themselves—honeysuckles, lilacs, jasmines, narcissi.

No one knows why a butterfly prefers a buddleia over a rose, except that buddleia does have a heavier scent, and butterflies do waft a delicious fragrance of their own, particularly on hot midsummer days. Honeysuckle, lavender, red valerian, Michaelmas daisy, verbena, and heliotrope are all flower nectars that butterflies love.

These flower scents attract suitors who in heights of romantic feelings are fooled into fertilizing the flowers instead of their female loves. Tiny white butterflies especially like cabbage plants (they lay about 100 eggs per plant), and red admiral butterflies are partial to *Sedum spectabile*. To have them in the garden is to have a bonus of beauty: naturalist Miriam Rothschild says it best in *The Butterfly Gardener:* "I garden purely for pleasure. I love plants and flowers and green leaves and I am incurably romantic—hankering after small stars spangling the grass. Butterflies add another dimension to the garden, for they are like dream-flowers—childhood dreams which have broken loose from their stalks and escaped into the sunshine." (There are colonies of moths called flatid bugs that come in red, white, green, even designer multicolors, and whenever they alight on a branch they arrange themselves so that their pattern looks exactly like a flower growing.)

Toads are other useful creatures to have around the garden. A toad can eat up to 8,000 insects in the space of twelve weeks. It also consumes grubs, rose chafers, squash bugs, tent caterpillars, armyworms, potato beetles, flies, and mosquitoes. To attract a friendly toad, put an inverted flowerpot (knock a hole into the side to make a door) in a sheltered place. Toads like warm dark places. Even a grapefruit shell, set on the ground with a doorway cut into its side, is good enough for a toad. However, it is probably easier to catch a toad than it is to attract one. (Send a child out to a waterhole with a net and a box.) Once you have your toad, fence him in so he can't go home again. Leave a piece of ripe fruit nearby to attract insects for him to eat and put some water in a pan a few inches deep, as he "drinks" through his skin. Once adjusted, the toad can be let out to go gobbling around the garden, eating every pest in sight. Just leave some water around for him, plus his dark little cavelike house.

More bulletins for peaceable kingdoms:

In nature, the more variation there is in plants, the better. Flowers, vegetables, and herbs grow well together (as they did in medieval gardens) because they mutually benefit each other.

Organic gardeners swear by these rules of planting:

- If you don't want butterflies to lay eggs on your cabbage leaves, then sage, rosemary, or thyme planted nearby will stop them.

- Nasturtiums will keep aphids off apple trees.

- Moths hate santolina.

- Roses grow better with a surrounding plant protection of garlic and parsley.

- If a hedge of buddleia and bee balm encloses a vegetable plot, most unwanted pests are excluded.

- Achillea (yarrow) is the doctor among plants, increasing their resistance to adverse conditions.

- An oak-leaf mulch on garden beds repels slugs and cutworms.

- Castor bean plants and sassafras keep away mosquitoes.

- Tansy and rue help keep away flies and so do nut trees.

- Spearmint and spurge (*Euphorbia lathryus*) repel mice and moles.

- Cats like *Nepeta cataria* (catnip or catmint—which is well known), but they also love *Centranthus ruber* (valerian). Earthworms like valerian too.

All this garden information comes from the *Premier of Companion Planting,* put out by the Bio-Dynamic Literature Company, P.O. Box 253, Wyoming, Rhode Island 02898.

GOODBYE WORLD

A refuge for birds, as well as a home for a hen, a dog, and a ferret, this Eden in New York State is called Goodbye World by its owner, who is an architect, a carpenter, and a gardener who dearly loves nature. Keeping a ferret is exotic enough, but having it get along with a dog and some chickens is truly astonishing. Even more astonishing is that they all play together like happy children. This proves that gardens can harbor birds and cats, dogs and llamas, wild and domestic fowl, or whatever pets take refuge in the natural scheme of all living things.

The garden is a bountiful expression of flower charms, with delphiniums, foxgloves, lilies, daisies, verbena, pansies, roses, and evening primroses all in full cry.

Looking back toward the handmade house, the garden plot shows the encircling birdhouses staked above its rustic fence. The gardener truly believes that a garden without birds would be a garden without a spirit.

Kimberly, the dog, is a gentle play-mate for Wissi Didi, although a cardboard roll is just as much fun (see page 9).

Wissi Didi, the ferret, likes to pose in a tub of verbena.

A fancy birdhouse swings high above a tangle of roses. The gardener actually raised a baby bird that had been abandoned by its mother. (The same bird often returns to the garden just to say hello.)

Henny Penny and her three little "Bumble Bees" feast on bread with cranberry sauce.

Every inch of space is used: here salad makings grow in tubs on the terrace.

Regina lives in Newport, Rhode Island, where she and her friends roam at will, very much at home in a garden bursting with flowers. The nonstop, color-all-the-way expanse is crammed with a good old-fashioned display of lots of plants, including delphinium, veronica, oenothera, and monarda; to the left in the foreground is the stylish *Allium sphaerocephalum,* known as the "drumstick" allium.

PETS
IN THE
GARDEN

On home grounds peaceable kingdoms can include all sorts of animals. To turn a corner in a garden and find a unicorn is a pretty tall order, but to come upon a llama is almost as surprising in these times. Amazingly, there are already around 7,000 llamas in this country. Their claim to fame is that they make great pack animals, but what is really newsy is that they are lovable pets and can even be housebroken (according to the National Llama Association). Some people like to have llamas as a part of their outdoor scenery for the same reason that others have shady glens and tranquil pools: serenity. A llama is a decorative animal that seems to exude repose.

May Day is a constant grazer in this Maine garden, happily munching the wild salad varieties that grow up to the grassy plateau. She never touches the serious border flowers that her friend Trudy grows so tenderly. (The deer get there first.)

Gardens should have a patch of Nepeta cataria for a cat to nip, as well as a nice shady pool for a dog to cool off in (even though he clashes with the pink and red astilbe).

A headline in The Wall Street Journal this summer read: "Some call llamas the cat's pajamas," and like thousands of others, this llama (called Butterskotch) is well trained and comes when her owner calls her; she is also a decorative part of the garden scenery and seems to have a positive aura of serenity.

SCULPTURED ANIMALS

This is not a plea for reproductions of pink flamingos on the front lawn or cast-iron cats on the roof, but for real sculptures of grace and distinction. So much statuary has passed through the gardens of history, and too often nowadays the statuary looks as if a carnival had landed on the lawn or the Greeks and Romans had done battle there.

This is a plea for animals in the garden, animals cast in bronze, and carved in wood and stone. Whether tame or wild, they seem to fuse with their natural surroundings and at the same time give them character. The sculptor's art is an added dimension that can be featured to add to a garden's entertainment, or tucked away as a surprise.

A Chinese dog is a staunch sentinel for showy rhododendrons.

Carrying on a family tradition, there are storks
on the roof (for good luck) and, just for fun,
a pig on the terrace.

A charming menagerie sculpted by Theodore Grosvenor is everywhere in the garden at Nearsea. For the curved border overlooking the ocean, a bushy white and pink Rosa rugosa hedge makes a green wall backdrop for the magnificent display of lilies.

A haughty sphinx is humbled by the common cultivar of black-eyed Susan, Rudbeckia fulgida 'Goldsturm,' a bloomer that begins in July and continues cheerfully until frost.

The little side garden with prancing cast-iron horses is a stylish vista planted to flow with the natural rock outcroppings. There are contrasting shades and shapes of greens with prostrate and upright junipers, variegated grasses, and sedums. Red pelargoniums and begonias are the exclamation points. (The staked sapling by the horse, near the quince, is a newly bought locust tree waiting for a permanent home.)

II.
On Design

Photograph by Ted Hardin

INSPIRATIONS: OPEN TO THE PUBLIC

The great big public gardens of America and certainly the great little gardens are bursting with ideas on design: seeing is believing, and no picture books can take the place of a visit. In Maine, the Asticou and Rockefeller gardens are inspiring; in Delaware, Winterthur is a glorious sight; on Long Island, the Old Westbury Gardens is a continuous joy. In New York, Wave Hill in the Bronx is a startling display all year around, and in Manhattan on upper Fifth Avenue, the Conservatory Garden in Central Park is a special delight. There are hundreds of botanical gardens, tropical gardens, historical gardens, arboretums, and greenhouses to explore. One of the greatest garden adventures for all kinds of plant environments is to visit The Duke Gardens Foundation of Somerville, New Jersey. There are eleven greenhouses to wander through, each expressing a different theme.

Headquarters for flower societies can also be exciting places to visit. The American Orchid Society has moved from Massachusetts to West Palm Beach, Florida, to the Vaughn estate, with six greenhouses open and a jungle-like garden on view. The Fairchild Tropical Gardens near Miami is another large botanic garden, beautifully landscaped and filled with exotic species of plants and trees.

The list of public garden places goes on and on, and to find more gardens with interesting and unusual plant collections, consult The Garden Club of America (598 Madison Avenue, New York, New York 10022), which puts out a paperback book of all the gardens open to the public throughout the country, a very useful guidebook to carry around on travels.

The Wave Hill Conservatory and the Wave Hill Thomas H. Everett Alpine House (located in the Bronx, overlooking the Hudson River) display a breathtaking wealth of flowering plants from Christmas on. These pictures (taken on the first day of spring) show the joyous profusion and creative staging of mass blooms.

One of the flower beds in the Conservatory Garden in Central Park at Fifth Avenue and 104th Street is of soft pastels, misted over with silver-gray artemisias, a sensitive composition of scale and color designed by Lynden B. Miller. Up the path in the foreground is purple catnip, a white peony, and white Siberian irises. The fluffy, rosy-pink mass is *Centranthus ruber,* a free-flowering self-seeder that blooms until fall. Winding throughout the beds are foxgloves and delphiniums in blues and pinks and white. The garden now has about 3,500 perennials, including four different varieties of perennial geranium: *Geranium platypetalum, G. sanguineum lancastriense, G.* 'Johnson's Blue,' and *G.* 'Wargrave Pink,' and meadow rue, *Thalictrum,* in three varieties: *T. rochebrunianum* or 'Lavender Mist,' *T. aquilegifolium,* and *T. speciosissimum glaucum.*

Also growing in abundance are phlox, daylilies, delphiniums, old roses, lilies, snakeroot, foxgloves, peonies, and four different species of iris. Some plants are in the gardens because of their distinctive foliage: hostas, liriope, and the beautiful, fuzzy gray *Salvia argentea.* In the fall, drifts of pink and white Japanese anemones and monkshood prolong the season.

Photograph by Ted Hardin

Three cheery yellows in a corner of the Wave Hill Conservatory: trained as a standard tree, Jasminum mesnyi; *next is* Cytisus canariensis; *the hanging basket holds sweet-smelling honey bells (*Hermannia verticillata*). Felicia, daisies, stock, and candelabra primulas mingle together to make winding paths of glorious color.*

The Abby Aldrich Rockefeller Garden, Mt. Desert, Maine, is a summer show from mid to late in the season, lavish with blooms.

Artemisia is the silver-gray frill that edges a double border showing a successful blend of peonies (not in bloom), yellow lilies, white daisies, red monarda, and pink achillea, with leather-leaved hostas dotted here and there.

FLOWER PLANS

One day, towards the end of September, I was sitting in the garden, making plans for next year. These plans, as each year passes by, become more elaborate, and incidentally more futile, because I always forget to look at them when the time comes.

The idea is to draw large squares in the garden notebook and label each square to represent a flower bed. Then one writes angry remarks in the squares.

At the moment in question I had written:

> *For the ninetieth time will you realize that you want masses and NOT clusters? The three clumps of red-hot pokers are just silly. They look extremely mean and slightly indecent.* YOU WANT AN ARMY OF RED-HOT POKERS.

I then licked my pencil, turned to the end of the book, and put down "order army of red-hot pokers."

Beverley Nichols, *A Village in a Valley*

And that's what happens in designing a garden: one or two plants are not enough. The dream is to have a garden furnished with a lavish hand, like a little Sissinghurst, charmed with plants in a tumble of blooms, with underplanting and intertwining and no bare soil to be seen anywhere. Beginning such a garden would be like furnishing a house: the trees and shrubs and vines are the backbone plantings (like sofas and chairs and beds), and the flowers are the added bibelots that give the place personality. Drifts of color make a flower border; not one, not two, but three plants that are alike make a group and five are even better. (Repetitions of plants give the border its fine balance.) Too many different plants will cause eyestrain: in furnishing a garden (as in furnishing a house) the result shouldn't look as if a whole furniture shop was emptied into the living room. According to all the gardening books *restraint, appropriateness, proportion,* and *color* are the guide words that lead to a pleasing design.

A good perennial garden needs air and sun and for best effect, some kind of backdrop, like a hedge, a fence, or a stone wall. In planning the border, count on six to eight feet of width for flowers and leave about one and one-half feet of space between the bed and its backdrop. (This gives circulation of air and will allow room for working from the back side.) This advice is for gardeners who have the space to allow, for if a border is six feet wide it has to be doubled in length (or more) for a pleasing proportion. And not every border has to have a backdrop; some can be better situated as free-flowing island beds in accordance with the lie of the land. But whatever the shape, whether rectangular or oval or like a gentle stream of blooms floating through a lawn, the plan can be committed to paper first. Look at pictures in catalogues, cut them out, and arrange them in a sequence that appeals to you.

You can arrange the plants on paper thus: Place the tallest at the back, left rear, then repeat the same plant in the center rear and the right rear of the bed. Fill in with the next tallest, and so on. Start with a list of favorites, such as:

Delphinium	36″–48″
Peony	24″–36″
Hemerocallis	30″–48″
Phlox	30″–36″
Aquilegia	30″
Iris	24″
Linum	18″
Salvia farinacea	18″–24″
Heuchera	18″–24″

Heights are the approximate mature sizes, and remember when you plant a perennial, the peak time of bloom and height is three years away.

Bloom time for the favorites listed is the following:

Late spring: *Aquilegia*
 Iris
 Peony

and sometimes overlapping

Early summer: *Delphinium*
 Heuchera (Both will bloom again later.)

Mid-to-late
summer: *Phlox*
 Hemerocallis
 Salvia (an annual in the North, a perennial in the South)

Ongoing
throughout
early-to-
late: *Linum*

The delphiniums and hemerocallis go to the back, the heucheras to the foreground, and as a lacing to entwine throughout the whole border: blue salvia (18 to 24 inches) and white linum (18 inches). Three, five, or better still, eight of the major plants for a long border make a grand enough showing to have harmonious blooms from late spring through September. If things don't go according to schedule, fill in with annuals or pots of blooms. The great Gertrude Jekyll used to drop pots of lilies and hydrangeas into her mixed border where some permanent plant had bloomed and then left a gap. Dahlias make good pot subjects, and they look perky and crisp and will stay in flower a long time, as will cleome (in pink, lilac, and white) and cosmos (in white to rose, flame red, and yellow).

The herb *Asperula odorata* (sweet woodruff) makes a nice edging for a mixed border (as do a lot of other herbs). This conventional plan is based on the premise that the wider and longer the planting is, the greater abundance of bloom and foliage. Another classic design is the double border flanking a broad central path, with one side banked against a backdrop and the other merging into lawn. An alternative popularized by the English designer Alan Bloom is the island bed that has all-around access, with the tallest growing plants placed near the center. For a relatively small island bed (18 by 9 feet), the tallest would run about three to four feet high.

A sample plan:

In the plan, blooms begin with iberis, campanula, dianthus, astilbe, and heuchera.

To have first blooms in whites (with a touch of blue in the edging plants), flower varieties would include:

Campanula cochleariifolia (C. pusilla): prolific from June to August, 5 inches high, thimble-sized bellflowers (lavender-blue to occasionally white) spreading to a tight mound 18 inches across.

Iberis sempervirens 'Autumn Snow': blooming in late May, early June, and when cut back will appear again in

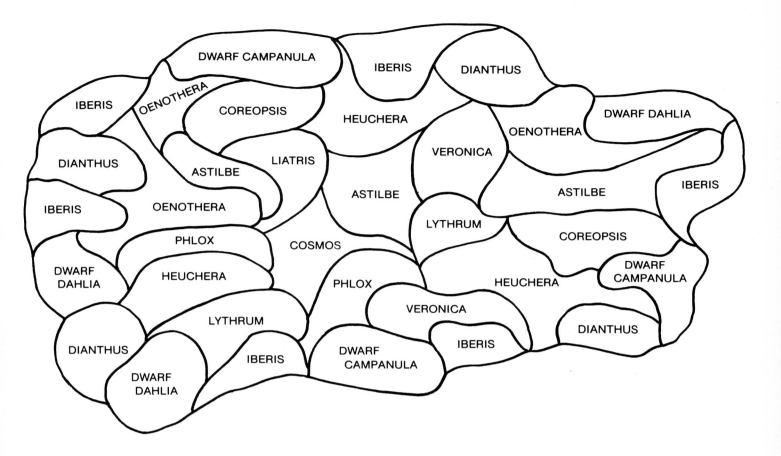

September and bloom again until frost, 9 inches high, with masses of white, star-shaped flowers.

Dianthus x *allwoodii* 'Blanche': fragrant blooms of clearest white from June until frost (flowers are a spectacular 1½ inches across), grows about 12 inches high.

Heuchera x 'White Cloud': June through September bloomer, about 18 inches high.

Astilbe x *arendsii* 'Avalanche': June into the middle of July performer, tallest flowering plant in the bed, about 30 to 36 inches, with purest white cascades of snowy plumes.

Coming after the initial bloom, with some overlapping, will be coreopsis, liatris, oenothera, and veronica.

Later: cosmos, dwarf dahlia, lythrum, and phlox.

On colors: coreopsis and oenothera come mostly in yellow; liatris blooms are purply-pink or white; lythrum comes in pink, purple, a deep carmine red, and a lighter rosy red. The border (mignon) dahlias are available in a large range: the white and yellow are the best. They are

all free-flowering (growing to about 15 inches) for an all-summer-long festival of bloom until the frost. The white is named 'Sneezy'; the yellow is called 'Irene van der Zwet.'

In June, after the flurry of white of campanula, dianthus, iberis (all flowering on the edge of the bed), the tall, dramatic astilbe, and the delicate little coralbells will come the rest of summer's blooms on into September: Yellows in oenothera and coreopsis (*Coreopsis verticillata* 'Golden Showers' grows about 24 inches high and is one of the few coreopsis that has attractive, fluffy foliage when it's out of bloom); veronicas (they can be light or dark blue, white or pink); phlox varieties are as white as popcorn or as red as wine and lots of shades in between, including the mauves and blues; the annual cosmos blooms in pinky-mauve and snow white with lacy, gossamer leaves.

Some sound advice on making flower plans comes from the McGourtys of Hillside Gardens in Norfolk, Connecticut. (Mr. McGourty is a former editor of the Brooklyn Botanic Garden's plant series *Plants and Gardens,* and he now grows about 700 species and cultivars of hardy perennials at his Hillside Gardens.) The

McGourtys garden six months of the year in the rigors of Zone 4 climate. Six good guidelines of theirs to follow:

1. Don't be afraid to experiment in your choice of plants or in how you use them.
2. Plant sizable clusters of the same plant and plant the beds full enough so that the foliage will eventually grow together to discourage the weeds.
3. Use colors that complement one another.
4. Place soft pastel colors and smaller plants closer to a terrace, and use bolder, larger blooms, farther away.
5. Plant white flowers and light, variegated foliage plants in darker, shady corners to bring the areas back into the garden.
6. Underplant species with flowers blooming in different seasons, like daffodils and violas followed by daylilies and daisies (*Heliopsis helianthoides* 'Incomparabilis').

A love-note cutting garden is in the shape of a single tear. With rocks as walls, it is filled with a tumble of flowers and herbs that look as if the birds and the bees planted it together. The heart in the center throbs with zinnias.

A border-in-the-round: triangular beds are set behind rolling mounds of lush boxwood. Aromatic herbs abound, intermingling with dwarf conifers in a color spectrum that is serene in purple, yellow, blue, and white.

Candy pinks are confections in a seaside garden contained within stone walls. The pinks-to-pales, so luminous at night, make a delectable bouquet: the display begins with roses, then follows with snapdragons, red nicotiana, pink Echinacea purpurea 'Bright Star,' an easy-to-grow coneflower. Just beyond are platycodon, lilies, and phlox. The right-hand border shows Malva alcea 'fastigiata' (hollyhock mallow).

The scallop-edged border is an ingenious device for turning a 150-foot-long stretch into a graceful garland. The spring blooms of dwarf astilbe, iris, early phlox, azaleas, and rhododendrons have just gone past; the hostas, daylilies, sedums, and echinops are soon to come.

Yellow is summer's charmer, the rays of gold that bring a gay spirit to the garden. The orange liliums fan the blaze, white daisies and phlox cool it.

COLOR

To pass through a cool enclosure of blues and grays to a glowing yellow and white garden can be like "sunshine after rain." The garden scene comes alive with color that creates atmosphere and mood.

In planning a design, color comes before outline. The first color in the garden is green. Every color looks great with green; it has to because that's the way nature made it happen. And because green is nature's most common color, it is the one color least noticed in a garden. The early Greeks believed that all matter was made up of four elements, and they gave each one a color: Earth was green; air was yellow; water, blue; and fire, red. Because the sun is the source of all color, yellow is the first important color and the closest to green. Yellow is warm and cheery and acts as a great stabilizer: a long border of yellow can be cooled and complemented with blue and white. Reds and oranges are the hottest colors. They are exciting and exotic in feeling, and for this reason the reds on the bluish side of the color spectrum are easier to place in the garden than the orangey-reds. Reds leap out at you and change perspective. Put red at the end of a border and the color seems to shorten the distance. In history one of the great red garden scenes ever painted is Claude Monet's *Terrace at Sainte-Adresse*, an absolute rage of red. Red flags are flying; borders bloom with red gladioli and orange nasturtiums; a center bed of hot geraniums is somewhat cooled with little dabs of white. And the most fantastic color note of all, which really carries the picture stylishly, is a red fence. The picture, reproduced in *The Enchanted Garden*, shows how red and green and white are exuberant in a setting.

Colors can clash when they are right next to one another (like red and yellow). Put a partition (such as white) between them, and the clash calms down. (It is the same principle as in medieval cloisonné work: putting black as a partition between brightly colored stained-glass fragments.) Red is a force in the garden, as it is in a sunset: when the sun is low on the horizon, it is seen through a long stretch of atmosphere, and when that happens, the blue of the sky scatters and the red comes through.

When the reds and magentas are too overpowering, they can be cooled and quieted with the pales of mauve and pink and white. White is as much a force as red, for although it is cool and quiet, it is also vibrant and fresh; it is probably the easiest single color to handle in a monochrome garden. And as color likes and dislikes are all so intensely personal, a garden can be a cacophony of color or a mild refrain. There is no rule that says that red and yellow absolutely have to have white as a buffer between them. So if purple and red and pink are your colors, they are fine for your garden too. Just as some people like pink socks with yellow sneakers, the preference is what makes personality and gives style.

Whatever colors are favored in the main design, sometimes an off-shade can add punch and interest to a too-perfect harmony, like a glow of hot orange next to a deep shade of magenta. The spectrum of combinations is limitless, but of all the colors there is one that stands out and is unique. Blue is the one color that melts and has the ability to lead the eye on and on to create the illusion of depth. Blue is also (along with green) the most natural color in nature.

Pink poppies and lavender irises were made for each other; they create a subtle and elegant atmosphere for a garden.

A single stroke of color, lightened by pink and pristine white, can dazzle a garden scene. Here, the brickwork, the terra-cotta pots, and a spill of velvet green lawn all work together to uphold the Mediterranean feeling of a red, red garden.

In a long border a punch of red lupines can stop the eye and foreshorten distance.

BLUES TO PURPLES

There are times when one's desire for blue is so intense that it must resemble the craving of the drunkard for a glass of whisky.

Beverley Nichols, *Laughter on the Stairs*

Heavenly blue flowers are the true blue bloods and aristocrats of the garden. They are called by so many names: hyacinth, sapphire, gentian, cobalt, delft, and on and on to describe their various blue shades, many of them borderline cases of mauve deepening into purple tinges. But whatever the hue, from the lightest and softest to the richest and deepest, they all do a special something that no other color can do in a particular setting. They provide the elegant touches that add glamour and aura to design.

For outstanding potent color the stately delphiniums command the toniest of all the blues, having a staggering and showy range of lush spires of flowers that bloom abundantly in early, mid, and late summer. And they hale from many diverse places. There is a delphinium from the Himalyas, *D. cashmerianum*; and one from Africa, *D. macrocentron*, a 24-inch plant of an intense shade of electric greenish blue. The Delphinium Society offers one of the rarest of all the species: *D. likiangense* from Yünnan province in China, which is coveted for the clearest blue color imaginable and having a lovely fragrance as well.

The following are blues of special merit:

Height	Scientific name	Description
24"–72"	*Delphinium cheilanthum formosum*	Garland dephinium with regal nickname: "Queen of the Border."
		Some noteworthy varieties are: 'Belladonna' - pale blue; 'Bellamosum' - dark blue; 'Cliveden Beauty' - light blue; 'Sapphire' - bright blue.

Next in producing beautiful blues, the campanulas follow the dephiniums and include some 300 species from lilliputians to 72-inch-high specimens. Some favorites are:

Height	Scientific name	Description
4″	Campanula cochleariifolia	Delicate, pale blue, with little bell-like blooms and a penchant for rock crevices.
9″–12″	Campanula carpatica 'Blue Chips'	Clear, sky-blue flowers shaped like platycodons, flowering from June through October in neat tufts.
12″	Campanula rotundifolia 'Olympica'	Deep blue bells in clusters, flowering from July through September, tidy and profuse.
24″–36″	Campanula persicifolia, e.g., 'Telham Beauty' (form of peach-leaved bellflower)	Exceptionally large true-blue flowers that bloom for many weeks in high summer on thin, wiry stalks.
60″–72″	Campanula lactiflora	A pale blue with flowers from late June to August.

More diverse blues, all perennial and all remarkably tolerant, are:

Height	Scientific name	Description
72″–108″	Omphalodes cappadocica	A woodland plant with intense blue flowers from late spring into early summer.
6″–12″	Gentiana septemfida lagodechiana	Leafy and low-growing with lovely deep blue bell-shaped flowers appearing through midsummer.
12″	Muscari 'Blue Spike'	Spectacular bright blue flowers with myriads of tiny blossoms blooming in early spring in clumps that colonize.
18″	Platycodon grandiflorum 'Mariesii'	Fragile-looking violet blue, single cup-shaped flowers.
12″	Chionodoxa luciliae	Big, star-shaped bright blue flowers in showy masses for early spring colonizing.
18″	Brunnera macrophylla	Likes dense shade and produces glorious bright blue flowers from late spring into early summer.
18″	Linum narbonense	Feathery, free-flowering with 1¾″ electric blue flowers on slender erect stems.
24″	Scabiosa caucasica 'Blue Perfection'	Poppylike 3″ blooms with cheerful, pale yellow centers, blooming June through September.
24″	Platycodon grandiflorum 'Double Blue'	A rich, true-blue, double-cup-shaped flowers opening from a balloon-shaped bud.
24″	Catananche caerulea 'Blue Giant'	Rare, cornflower-blue blossoms with spiky petals and indigo centers, from June through September.

Height	Scientific name	Description
24″	*Tradescantia* x *andersoniana* 'Blue Stone'	Summerlong performer with solid blue pansylike flowers growing out of long, strappy, narrow leaves.
24″	*Centaurea montana*	Deeply cut flowers of rich cornflower blue and silvery gray foliage, an all-summer-long performer.
30″	*Echinops* 'Taplow Blue'	Spectacular thistles of deep intense blue, from July to October.
30″	*Cynoglossum nervosum*	Profusions of gentian-blue flowers, like large forget-me-nots on erect well-branched stems.
30″	*Veronica* 'Blue Charm'	Deep blue flower spikes, often 15″ long, bloom all summer long. There are also: 'Crater Lake Blue,' a deep gentian-blue; 'Heavenly Blue,' a mat-forming variety; and 'Blue Peter,' in deep, almost navy blue.
36″	*Aster frikartii* 'Wonder of Staffa'	Radiant hyacinth-blue flowers 2½″ across, blooming in profusion from June until frost.
36″–48″	*Baptisia australis*	Racemes of blue flowers bloom on stalks rising from elegant gray-green leaves.

Delphinium, the "Queen of the Border," always stands in command from the back of the flower bed. Some varieties are blue-to-purple giants that grow to be over seven feet tall. ▶

The silver grays can lace through a flower bed, keeping a full house of eclectic blooms in good order. Here the artemisia is a foil for Achillea millefolium 'Fire King' (yarrow).

DESIGNING WITH FOLIAGE

Plants that are strappy, grassy, moundy, feathery, fluffy, lacy, whatever; plants with "handsome foliage" or "distinctive leaves": there are hundreds of beautiful varieties listed and shown in plant catalogues; and putting together which leaves go with what can be either great fun or a great chore, according to your inclination. A lot of gardeners grow flowers they love and just let the leaves fall where they may, but professional landscape gardeners count leaves and pay a lot of attention to their shapes: palmate, pinnate, peltate, linear, lanceolate, and lobed are all leaf shapes and forms that have a lot to do with the looks of a plant. Those with stalky, strappy leaves (linear) can match well with plant leaves that are full and round or full and heart-shaped (cordate). Not to put too fine a point on leaf-matching, there are two categories of plants with leaves more interesting than their blooms. They make strong and interesting statements in the garden: the silver grays and the variegated ones.

THE SILVER GRAYS

Silver-gray-leaved plants are especially magical. In summer they look crystalline and cool, gleaming in the moonlight and glimmering in sunshine; and their leaves wear coatings that look like velvet or silk, wax or wool, a natural protection against harsh winds and dry spells. These hardy and perennial silver grays are the background clouds that diffuse too hot (or too exuberant) a color scheme in the garden. They act as sensible anchors to hold *down* a flower border: their powdery leaf shades can work as the strong connector between too diverse or too eclectic colors.

The romantic artemisias, delightfully feathery and easy to grow, are some of the handsomest silvery grays, able to create atmosphere and establish order in a garden. There are many species and varieties: *A. lactiflora* and *A. abrotanum* grow about 48 to 60 inches high; *A. ludoviciana* 'Silver King,' *A. arborescens*, and *A.* 'Lambrook Silver' grow about 36 to 48 inches tall; *A. schmidtiana* 'Nana' is a low mound suitable for the front of the garden (or a rockery), as it grows up to 12 inches. More perennial silver grays to act as stars in the flower border are particular standouts, but with all their outstanding foliage the flowers they produce are often insignificant.

Height	Scientific name	Description
4"–6"	*Stachys olympica (S. byzantina)* 'Silver Carpet'	Soft, furry, and mat-forming, a nonflowering variety.
6"–8"	*Chrysanthemum (Tanacetum) haradjanii*	A mounded carpet of leaves looking exactly like tiny feathers, having a sharp scent when bruised, and producing groundsellike yellow flowers (best removed, for they detract from the beautiful foliage).
6"–9"	*Cerastium tomentosum*	Forms dense mats of silvery, whitish leaves, with tiny, white flowers.
8"	*Dianthus Danielle*	Pinky-coral flowers, looking as if they were watercolors, rise out of gracefully curving, spiky leaves of powdery gray.
8"	*Anthemis marschalliana*	Tiny, daisylike yellow flowers blooming out of moundlike silvery-gray, feathery foliage.
8"–10"	*Santolina chamaecyparissus* 'Nana'	A dwarf shrub with close-packed silver-gray foliage and yellow, daisylike flowers.
12"	*Veronica incana*	Sprawling habits, making clumps of pointed leaves below deep, purple-blue spiky flowers.
12"–24"	*Convolvulus cneorum*	Silky-white or pinkish flowers bloom in late spring to summer, shaped rather like morning glories with yellow centers. Hardy only in South.
18"	*Anaphalis margaritacea*	Puffy, white popcornlike flowers appear in late summer above elegant ribbed leaves.
18"–24"	*Ballota pseudodictamnus*	A sprawling, clump-forming shrub with neat, crisply rounded leaves of a subtle silvery gray. The mauve flower that blooms in midsummer is not pretty.
36"–48"	*Senecio laxifolius*	A handsome shrub that forms dense mounds of gray-green leaves outlined in white; its yellow flower is best pinched out. Not hardy in northern climes.
36"–48"	*Thalictrum aquilegifolium*	A Columbine-leafed elegant, airy plant with tiny pink, pufflike clouds of flowers rising out of softest gray-green foliage.
60"–96"	*Macleaya microcarpa* and *M. cordata*	The grayish foliage is wonderfully lobed, veined, and distinctive, and flowers are plumes of softest pink or white.
60"–96"	*Buddleia fallowiana* 'Alba'	A bushy plant with fragrant, creamy white flowers that spill over their stems in graceful sprays.

VARIEGATED LEAVES

Plants with variegated leaves make dramatic exclamation points; they can also be massed on their own to make strong gestures. Although they usually lack a full complement of chlorophyll (which is apt to cause fragility), they are stalwarts (surprisingly enough) and the ones listed here are amazingly adaptable to many adverse conditions.

Hostas are the leading lights of the variegated look, and nurseries with a wide range of perennials will offer at least a dozen varieties. They grow as great ground-covering clumps of leaves, and even though they like a moisture-retentive soil and partial shade, they can combat poor soil and dryish conditions. ("Volunteer" hostas have suddenly appeared in my rock garden, which is more rock than garden, and they are holding on with true-grit stamina.)

The following variegated-leaf plants are perennial, particularly good-looking, and remarkably care-free. They make spectacular accent plants when grouped in mass plantings; or they can be effective in small doses, like dabs of light on a dark canvas.

Height	Scientific name	Description
3″–4″	Ajuga reptans 'Variegata'	Tight foliage forms a neat carpet with delightful blue flower panicles in late spring and early summer.
12″	Pittosporum tobira 'Variegata'	Has clusters of white flowers and thick, cream-speckled leathery leaves about 4″ long.
12″–18″	Arum italicum 'Pictum'	Strongly defined, creamy-veined leaves in an interesting, speckled pattern. The white flowers are short-lived and nondistinctive and are followed by spikes of orangey-red berries.
24″	Hosta crispula	Lovely creamy silver variegation on rather leathery leaves, with elegant lavender flowers in midsummer.
24″	Molinia caerulea 'Variegata'	Forms densely tufted clumps of graceful, grasslike leaves that have cream margins.
24″	Liriope muscari 'Variegata'	Grasslike foliage has yellow stripes; the lilac-purple flowers bloom in September.
30″	Lunaria annua 'Variegata'	The striking foliage is heart-shaped with fuzzy edges outlined in white; reddish flowers bloom in late spring to midsummer.
36″	Iris pallida 'Variegata'	Striped foliage and lavender-blue to white flowers; blooms in May or June.
36″	Polygonatum odoratum 'Variegatum'	Graceful foliage, edged in white, and leaf stalks producing demure bell-shaped flowers that look rather like gigantic lilies of the valley.

and two shrubs of note:

Height	Scientific name	Description
72″–96″	Euonymus japonica 'Aureo-variegata'	Has large leaves blotched with gold in the center.
72″–96″	Euonymus japonica 'Microphyllus variegatus'	Shows white-margined leaves.

Leaves with extravagant markings are design elements that compel the eye to stop and take notice.

Behind stone walls fields of rudbeckias wave a yellow-and-green swath of a path down to the sea. Rudbeckias, a much-improved cultivar of black-eyed Susans, keep blooming from July through October, a reliable long-term treat.

GOOD IDEAS

Landscape designers are knowledgeable in the ways of designing with plants to create style in the garden. Some of their ideas are unexpected in the use of unusual combinations mixing plant materials and colors—but all of them are visually exciting and can be easily imitated.

The following ideas are planned from a broad range of designs:

- For a shady entrance, a border of green nicotiana;

- Along a sunny driveway, a hedge of sunflowers (the U.S. record for sunflower height is 17 feet)—just imagine that bordering a driveway!;

- Planted in rum keg tubs on the edge of a terrace, squash plants;

- To edge a path, gerbera daisies alternating with the dwarf version of fountain grass (*Pennisetum*);

- In clumps in front of an entrance, *Echinops Ritro* 'Taplow Blue' matched with *Gypsophila paniculata* (baby's breath);

- Planted in big terra-cotta pots and placed as sculptures around a swimming pool, *Allium giganteum*;

- A walkway outlined with a hedge of *Rodgersia podophylla;*

- Laburnums (which are extremely hardy) trained to climb up a trellis or treated as a wall shrub;

- To liven up a corner of a garden that needs a seasonal perk: different ornamental grasses, of different heights, planted in various sizes of terra-cotta pots;

- A garden bench of stone, planted with creeping thyme to make a soft, scented cushion;

- Clethra trained to grow over a pergola for a sweet-smelling shelter;
- *Phillyrea latifolia*, a scented hedge used as a backdrop for a kitchen garden;
- The quick-growing fig vine trained into "ropes" to form a trellis pattern against a wall;
- A border edging-hedge of germander for a herb garden will have blooms of pale pink to entice the honeybees and can be kept sheared off for compact neatness;
- For a terrace, an aromatic hedge of alternating gray and green lavender cotton (*Santolina chamaecyparissus* and *Santolina virens*);
- To define the borders of a small enclosed garden, a wall of pleached (entwined or interlaced) pittosporum trees underplanted with variegated ivy.

There are so many ideas for garden styles, and here are more from Julie Morris, an ardent gardener who is the horticulturist on the staff of Blithewold Gardens and Arboretum in Bristol, Rhode Island:

- Try growing *Plumbago auriculata (F. capensis)*, a popular terrace plant, as a standard. The plants bloom from late summer until frost and are a lovely sky blue.
- The annual Dahlberg daisy with its feathery foliage and tiny, clear yellow flowers is an ideal plant to spot between flagstones on a terrace. It also thrives planted along the edges of gravel paths. (Collect seeds each year for the following season.)
- Plant the low-growing barberry 'Crimson Pygmy' along the top of stone retaining walls or against a weathered grey fence; the color is striking against shades of grey. (It is especially useful in seaside areas where it sparkles on foggy days.)
- Grow the shrub *Caryopteris* 'Blue Mist' in your herbaceous border or cutting garden. The fluffy blue flowers on arching branches are wonderful for cutting. The shrub is in bloom from mid-August until frost.
- Try planting *Didiscus caerulea*, the blue lace flower, in combination with *Nicotiana* 'Nicki Green,' or one of the other lime-green hybrids. The combination is unusual and striking.
- Fence an herb and vegetable garden with cordoned fruit trees for beauty and an additional crop.

- Don't be afraid to use some spot of red in your garden; its brightness will show off all the subtleties of the paler shades.
- Plant flowers near the terrace for evening fragrance: stock, nicotiana, heliotrope, and mignonette.
- A small garden will appear larger if the borders, rather than paralleling one another along each side of a garden path, start to come together in the distance—ever so slightly.

Julie Morris writes about her own delightful garden in Newport, Rhode Island, and for inspiration for gardeners everywhere:

During the gardening season I spend most of my time taking care of other people's gardens. In general, our clients prefer lots of color in the flower borders we maintain. Perhaps, as a reaction to all this color, I have chosen to use a great deal of white flowering plants in my own garden areas. The effect is restful, and, because I am rarely at home during the day, I can enjoy the white and other pale colored flowers well into the evening.

By mid-summer the white petunias I plant each year have cascaded down the sides of their strawberry jar container. The large pot sits under the flowering crab apple at the end of the path leading from the front gate. The fragrant white flowers work their magic in early evening when they almost shimmer. Viewed from the front gate they are a beacon of restfulness after a long day of gardening.

I look forward to coming home through the garden gate every day to see what new flower has opened. I plan for fragrance as well as flowers, so starting with the March blooming *Daphne mezereum* all the way through the seasons until the fragrant *Elaeagnus pungens* blooms in fall there is something filling the air with its perfume.

I planted most of the fragrant shrubs in the border along the path that runs from the front gate to the backyard. The *Magnolia virginiana* is planted right next to the steps leading to the back door. It blooms on and off throughout the summer, filling the evening air with its sweet scent.

Another important aspect of my planning was that I would be able to enjoy my plants on the run. Some days I only have time to catch a glimpse of what is happening in the garden. These glimpses are my "small moments" in the garden and perhaps involve the most important part of my garden planning.

Favorite horses are commemorated with gravestones, and the area is planted with a low-maintenance garden of floribunda roses, sedums, and prostrate junipers.

An ornamental slat-house makes a stylish entrance to a vegetable garden, and in the summer provides a cool place for orchid plants. The white Agapanthus orientalis *'Albus' is a design feature to complement the owner's horse.*

A few years ago I was sitting on the back steps and could see out of the corner of my eye a very pleasing sight. The lemon-yellow daylily 'Hyperion' was blooming in front of a dusty pink monarda. For many days I would glimpse this particular combination as I went about my work. I realized that most of the combinations I liked best in the garden were viewed this way; the pale blue plumbago growing in a pot next to an apricot colored verbena, a white clematis growing in and around the mock orange, and the one true potpourri of the garden, the raised bed with its mixture of colorful annuals, herbs and vegetables.

In addition to enjoying the plants in my garden, I share the space with the four cats and two dogs. I enjoy watching the animals and am again reminded of Gertrude Jekyll's comment that cats were the perfect companions in her garden.

We recently hired an arborist to prune the large Norway maple in the yard next door. The tree's canopy has been thinned out and now interesting patterns of sunlight dance around on the borders below its shade. The light sets off the colors of the flowers and the texture of the foliage, creating movement yet somehow unifying the tone of the garden.

The kind of gardening I like to do best involves far more than the use of a variety of plants. I choose plants for the color and tone and use the natural light and shade in the garden to enhance their texture and form. Creative gardening sets the mood necessary to sustain the soul. These "small moments" in the garden do indeed make a lifetime much more pleasant.

The following is Julie Morris's choice of trees and shrubs selected for fragrance:

> *Chionanthus virginicus* — fringetree
> *Daphne burkwoodii* 'Carol Mackie'
> *Daphne burkwoodii* 'Somerset'
> *Daphne mezereum* — February daphne
> *Elaeagnus pungens* —thorny elaeagnus
> Exbury hybrid azaleas
> *Magnolia virginiana* — sweet bay
> *Philadelphus virginalis* 'Glacier'
> *Rhododendron (Azalea) arborescens*
> x *Rhododendron (Azalea) 'Daviesii'*
> *Rhododendron mucronatum (Azalea ledifolia alba)*
> *Rhododendron (Azalea) viscosum*
> *Syringa palibiniana* — dwarf Korean lilac
> *Syringa prestoniae* 'James McFarlane'
> *Viburnum carlesii*

Rooms-within-rooms in a garden spot that is a decorative tour de force: a grove of laburnum trees are crisply edged with lilies of the valley and bright poppies. To get the most out of the space, a small salad garden is inched into one corner.

A pocket-size front-door garden looks as pretty as a miniature painting and shows great artistry in design. Nancy McCabe, the artist who planned and planted it, wanted an easy-care and informal arrangement. There are foxgloves in clay pots, dianthus, Canterbury bells, and sweet Williams dotted among herbs. Trained into standard trees on either side of the garden bench is heliotrope. Alchemilla (lady's-mantle) is in the left foreground looking a little flattened after a rain shower, but the plant will perk up again and bloom with yellowish-green flower panicles practically all summer. The low-growing splash of bright canary yellow in the background is oenothera (evening primrose), an extremely hardy plant.

For a special little girl, a remembrance garden has a serene and graceful spirit, filled with nicely scaled plants given by those who knew and loved the child. The glossy-leafed edging around the pond is European wild ginger (Asarum europaeum), a perfect edging for shady spots.

An idea for combining the best of both worlds: a
welcoming front garden, formal with roses and
boxwood and yet cottagey with an old-fashioned
border marching along the brick wall perimeters.
Peony plants form a hedge of glossy foliage; the
annuals and perennials are in a mixed planting
behind the clipped periwinkle edging.

The garden as architecture, a unifying link to bind new buildings with old in a pleasing and dignified design. The new gazebolike structures are (1) a bath connected to the colonnaded end of the house, and (2) a freestanding office pavillion for a busy executive. The garden is alight with sunny rudbeckias, hollyhocks, cosmos, and daisies, all arranged around ornamental center beds planted with dwarf snapdragons.

A swimming pool, looking as if it popped out of the ground like the natural surrounding rocks, is framed by a field of wild daisies—a lovely way of extending and bordering the country setting.

Lynden B. Miller, the director and restorer of the Conservatory Garden of Central Park, designed her own garden to hide a swimming pool. Beyond the yew hedge the land has been bulldozed to change the perspective, and the rose arbor is deliberately placed off-center to lead the eye to the right. In the 150-foot-long border the flowers are anchored by a myriad of gray and green textures and shapes, like the warp and weft of tapestry weaving. The flowing pattern of plants and flowers in front of the precisely clipped hedge is a clever foil to turn what was an unsightly view into an intimate garden.

To the left of the rose arbor is a variegated dogwood shrub (*Cornus alba* 'Elegantissima variegata') and below is a silver-gray dwarf blue spruce. Sedum, catmint, artemisia, and lady's-mantle make compact mounds for fronting the border. On the right side, twinkling in the sunlight, is a *Geranium* 'Johnson's Blue.' The soft yellow shrub to the right is *Potentilla fruticosa* 'Katherine Dykes,' which thrives in any soil, in sun or partial shade, from June until frost.

A front entrance to an old New England house is blanketed with a canopy of creeping thyme (Thymus serpyllum 'Coccineus'). It makes another bright fling draped down stone stairs. This variety is extremely hardy and can be planted in small niches in hot, dry places for early summer color.

An inviting front path meanders through purple veronicas, yellow African daisies, and bouquets of fluffy white gypsophila. The punch of red is astilbe; the blooming pink and pale yellow honeysuckle spilling over the fence is Lonicera heckrottii 'Goldflame.'

An enclosed garden that marches in steps down from a stone terrace cascades blooms: roses bank far walls, tall pink lythrum dominates the left corner, pink liatris holds the opposite one. The rich purples are vigorous tradescantia (spiderwort), an all-summer-long bloomer with beautiful long narrow leaves.

III.
*Black
Thumb
Thoughts*

GREAT
PERFORMERS

Here was I, craving for a garden, with the sap dying in
me and the last traces of green fading from my fingers.
Beverley Nichols, *Merry Hall*

All gardeners who have the knack of making things grow will no doubt not be interested in the subject of "black thumbs," but for a lot of us it is a major concern. We are beginners who worry about what plants look best with others, what plants should go where, and how to mix and match colors, which plants are tender and which are tough. In short, we have doubts not only of our ability to make things grow but also to make something visually appealing. These "black thumb thoughts" can be very inhibiting to any gardener who is just beginning to get the feel of the good earth between his fingers. One very good solution, besides devouring gardening books and going on garden tours, is to study catalogues. They are supremely helpful in assuaging fears about soil and light requirements, heights and habits, and times and types of blooms. Here are descriptions of the same plant from three different catalogues:

White Flower Farm:
   CIMICIFUGA (sim-me-siff-you′ga) **Ranunculaceae.** Snakeroot. Tall border plants that grow in ordinary soil in sun or part shade. They have large leaves and plume-like branching flower spikes. Varieties are difficult to find, but not scarce, just difficult for nurserymen to propagate. Sometimes we can't get them started, either. But they are not the least hard for you to grow and are hardy in *Zones 3 to 9.*

   C. racemosa. Handsome, very long racemes of white flowers. The leaves grow to 3 feet and the flower

spikes may grow to 6 or 7 feet. So under good culture it grows high and is for the back of the border. Once established it stays. The root, if you care, is used medically as a sedative.

Spring Hill:
   CIMICIFUGA Impressive 4′ spires composed of myriad tiny pearl white florets stand tall in back of your perennial border. Cimicifuga is noted not only for its lovely blossoms but also its graceful leaves, which sometimes reach as long as 2′. A highly valuable garden plant, it stands proudly and never fails to capture attention, even in shady spots to which it's ideally suited. Also superb for cut flower bouquets.*Cimicifuga racemosa*

Wayside Gardens:
   CIMICIFUGA racemosa—**Snakeroot** Handsome, shade loving plants that bloom in July and August, with 4 to 6 foot spikes of pure white flowers. Splendidly suited to the back of the border or for naturalizing at the edge of woods. Zones 4–9.

So from reading the three descriptions and looking at the gorgeous pictures, you gather that this is a dramatic, superb plant that would do fine in a sunny or a shady spot. And you see the truth of the matter is that plant preferences need not be taken too awfully seriously. That's not to say that cimicifuga would grow taller and

*Tart pink yarrow is a lively mix with purple salvia and yellow oenothera and makes a
harmonious picture paired with the fuzzy-edged red monarda.*

look even grander given perfect conditions, but it will still grow given not-so-perfect conditions. That's true for many plants. Say you notice *Thalictrum dipterocarpum*, a species of meadow rue, in the back of someone's very sunny border and it looks perfectly happy. In fact it is so happy it stands about 96 inches tall. Reading up on meadow rue you find that the plant loves shade, rich soil, plenty of moisture, and grows to about 60 inches tall. It sounds like a full-time job just keeping the thalictrum fed with the sprinkler turned on it all the time. The fact is the plant is not a bit fussy; it can withstand sun, wind, and drought. Hostas are the same way. They are touted as shade-loving perennials, but they will grow anywhere, in any type of soil. They are also long-lived, never need transplanting or spraying, and so for black thumbs they are absolutely foolproof. One of the showiest of the hostas is 'Royal Standard,' with lovely, scented white flowers on stems about 24 inches tall and a bloom time that begins in late August and lasts for about three weeks. This stately plant can weather anything.

It is astounding that some of the most beautiful (and useful) plants are the most tolerant and easiest to grow. Lonicera (honeysuckle) grows anywhere, in any kind of soil and in the most exposed places. It can be trained and pruned into a standard tree, espaliered against a wall in a controlled shape, or the branches may just be left to ramble over fences and rocks. Boltonia is another nonchoosy perennial winner that grows in either damp or dry places. *B. asteroides* 'Snowbank' looks like a fluffy hedge of delicate white daisies on 36- to 48-inch sprays that never need staking. Even light frosts don't daunt the flowers.

Gardeners call these perennial wonders "great performers" and they deserve the accolades. They cover a wide range of bloom, from early summer through September, and some are cut-and-come-again varieties, which means if they bloom early and are cut to the ground, they will come back again in late summer full of renewed vigor and high color. "Tough as a ginkgo" is another expression to describe them: for 150 million years the ginkgo species has been reproducing in a basically unaltered form, which says everything for its adaptability. Plants *do* have a will to live. They renew themselves from their own tissues: bulbs make offsets; strawberries send out runners; poppies scatter their seeds to the wind; irises multiply rhizomes, all of them increasing by their own devices.

The following is a very personal list of great performers. They have all done well by the sea, in the wind, and through drought and huge neglect. For all the foregoing reasons this is a list of survivors for black thumbs to note:

Achillea	Hemerocallis
Alchemilla	Heuchera
Astilbe	Hosta
Baptisia	Liatris
Boltonia	Lythrum
Campanula	Malva
Catananche	Oenothera
Centaurea	Physostegia
Centranthus	Rudbeckia
Cimicifuga	Scabiosa
Coreopsis	Thalictrum
Dictamnus	Veronica
Geranium	

Peonies are lovely lush blooms accompanying distinctive irises in a border.

GOOD
COMPANIONS

Certain plants are good companions: they contrast with or complement each other with their colors, their leaf formations, and their growing habits. They have a certain interaction and play, and put alongside each other in amiable clumps, they make charming pictures together. A way of keeping a visual notebook of good companions is to cut pictures from catalogues and paste them alongside each other. The ones listed here have natural affinities for each other; their attributes are alike and yet different at the same time, for in some cases opposites attract:

Cynoglossum nervosum (Chinese forget-me-not) blooms for weeks and weeks in the middle of summer on erect stems that branch out well and reach about 30 inches high. The gentian-blue flowers make a distinct background for *Coreopsis verticillata* 'Grandiflora,' which grows 24 inches tall and shows masses of yellow daisylike flowers spilling over lacy, finely cut leaves. The bloom is from June to September.

Another upright presence for the border, which grows shrublike (up to 30 inches tall), is *Dictamnus albus* (gas plant), an all-month-long June bloomer with handsome, finely divided leaves and honeysucklelike pure white or soft pink flowers in spikes. *Linum perenne* (flax) is a pretty accompaniment with its luminous, clear blue flowers blooming all summer long on 18-inch stems with feathery blue-green leaves.

Platycodon grandiflorum (balloon flower) blooming in deep blue violet on 20-inch stems looks very fetching with *Thalictrum dipterocarpum* (meadow rue) with its soft rosy-mauve flower sprays. It grows over 36 inches tall and blooms in late summer on stems with beautiful aquilegia-shaped gray-green leaves. Platycodon tend to be stridently stalkly (but with crisply defined leaves) and they make a perfect marriage with the graceful thalictrums, whose style is all airy-fairy.

Centranthus ruber 'Roseus' is a rewarding plant that not only has pretty rosy-red flower clusters from June to frost, but it will withstand any kind of soil and either sun or partial shade. Known commonly as red valerian, the plant grows about 24 inches high with rich green foliage. A likely mate for this beauty is the pink false dragonhead, *Physostegia virginiana* 'Vivid,' a June through September bloomer that grows upright to about 20 inches high. (The flower spikes look like miniature digitalis.)

Salvia nemorosa 'East Friesland' is another all-summer-long delight with 18-inch spires of intense purple. This also would make a wonderful foil for centranthus and physostegia.

Linaria genistifolia looks like a lemon-yellow snapdragon with a long tail. It grows into a full mound about 30 inches high, blooming in late May through July. It is of low-maintenance and is self-sowing. With a complement of *Salvia* 'Blue Queen' the plant makes a fantastic picture (salvia grows to 24 inches tall and blooms in deep violet blue).

Soft touches to lighten up the boldness of pink *Liatris spicata* 'Kobold': blue *Scabiosa caucasica* and white *Scabiosa caucasica* 'Alba,' two exquisite blooms that look airborne and as fragile as lace. They flower in early July and last until late August with flower heads that are up to 3 inches across. *Liatris pycnostachya* (gayfeather) is regal, about 24 inches in height, and flowers from July to September.

Landscape designer Priscilla Williams uses these favorite plant combinations to make good companions for her garden designs:

- Daylily 'Singing Sixteen' (a rosy apricot color) with chelone (a rosy pink turtlehead plant), and *Ligularia* 'Desdemonia,' a purply-leaved plant.

- *Hosta sieboldiana* 'Elegans,' as a companion with the deep rose daylily 'Haunting Melody,' along with pink and white astilbe, lobelia, and the Japanese silver-painted fern *Athyrium goeringianum.*

- *Anemone sylvestris* and *Viola cornuta* 'Jersey Gem.'

- Pale pink daylily 'Bambi Doll,' *Hosta* 'August Moon,' and *Astilbe chinensis pumila* (raspberry color), with blue stokesia, silver lamb's ears, white veronicas and *Aster* 'Elma Potschke,' a shocking-pink shade.

Shades of pinks, fuchsias, and pungent wine reds bloom in high summer along with daisies, cosmos, and petunias, all edged with snowy sweet alyssum. Delphinium, foxglove, phlox, and baby's breath are the perennials that serve as the backbone of this border.

Deep purple-blue delphinium and clear pink lythrum spires pair up with bright yellow coreopsis and soft-toned snapdragons.

This beguiling street border is spiced with pink and red hollyhocks and yellow yarrow. The purply-blue flower is Adenophora confusa, *a July and August bloomer that looks very much like campanula.*

Veronica latifolia *'Crater Lake Blue'* *with its spires of deep gentian blue and* Lilium *'Enchantment'* *in magnificent orange look especially fetching combined with the airy cosmos.*

A fiesta of pink lychnis and yellow marigolds—Lychnis viscaria 'Flore-pleno' blooms
vibrantly in June and July and will seed itself; its leaves turn almost crimson in the fall.

The play of satiny lilium and deep blue platycodon

*Heavenly scented lavender
and tart pelargonium*

Siberian iris and creamy astilbe

THE
DO-NOT-DISTURB
PERENNIALS

Some perennials just like to stay in the same spot and grow old together; so they should be left alone:

Aconitum   Incarvillea
Adenophora   Kniphofia
Aquilegia   Lavandula
Artemisia   Limonium
Asclepias   Linum
Bapitisia   Liriope
Dictamnus   Malva
Eryngium   Mirabilis
Filipendula   Nepeta
Gentiana   Peony
Geranium   Platycodon
Gypsophila   Salvia
Helleborus   Santolina

Some perennials can be dug up and divided to start new plants; these can be separated in the spring or fall:

Aruncus   Hosta
Cimicifuga   Polygonum
Epimedium   Sedum
Euphorbia   Thalictrum
Hemerocallis

Planting advice to remember: always throw a scant handful of long-acting fertilizer into the hole when planting perennials in the fall. Then, too, there is this advice from Thalassa Cruso in *Making Things Grow Outdoors:* "My notion is not to be bullied too much by my plants." A good nurseryman in Rhode Island, when asked about planting instructions, replied, "Plant it, water it, weed it."

IV.
Intimate Worlds

The gazebo is a garden-within-a-garden, a show-house for tuberous begonias and a sparkling fresh flower arrangement.

GARDEN
OPEN TODAY

The house is decorated with fragrant orchids, peonies, and roses, clustered and arranged in sprays, and one wanders among this splendid show of blooms in a kind of color haze, walking through rooms full of delicate scents. It is the first act in a grand performance of many more excitements to come. The festive flowers spill over and out of the house to merge with generous terraces that shelter under giant 100-year-old live oak trees spreading through the vista like a miniforest. Beyond these curtains of green the garden unfolds with a party box full of surprises: the scene has a holiday air, as if flags were flying and banners proclaiming "garden open today," and indeed it is a favorite garden tour for Main Liners.

The jubilation of flowers, always at peak bloom times, begins in beds around the swimming pool and the gazebo, then moves on up through various raised plateaus and levels of lawn. The finale is The Folly, the rotunda greenhouse with its appendages that are a celebration and combination of hot houses, orangeries, tree houses, conservatories, and cutting gardens—truly a Victorian extravaganza. The year-round in-house enticements are rampant with towering bamboos and palms, tropical vines, specimen trees, a collection of miniature orchids, and more ongoing cutting flowers, row-on-row mixed with a full enrichment of unusual potted plants in constant bloom. (These are on the move, and go in and out of favor, as they are whisked into the house for stardom, and when they dim, new lights take their places.)

Outside the flower beds keep up the pace with their array of color: after irises, lupines, columbines, and coral bells dwindle, the orange and yellow lilies and snapdragons take the stage. The late summer gleams are white phlox that glow luminously in the dark; then come chrysanthemums in whites and yellows and lavenders, with a final florish of dark winy red ones energetically flowering around Thanksgiving time. (Throughout the garden the delphiniums contribute a lot to the nonstop color; they take a deep breath after each cutting and bloom twice more during the season.)

By rotating plants in high performance, the winter season never seems to come around. Spring is always singing forth inside the house and is an early herald outside, with lots of bulbs to enliven the garden. This is a cultivated world of sweeping gestures, beautifully orchestrated, and like any special treat that everyone looks forward to it is a year-long event of gorgeous blooms that mercifully neither rain, nor sleet, nor snow could ever spoil.

Triumphant lupines are like sentinels in front of the dancing blooms of Heuchera x brizoides *'Pluie de Feu' (coralbells).*

Potted nasturtiums are tucked into the arms of the old oak tree and then arranged like a riot of color on a tiered garden stand.

A cool terrace is cloistered by 100-year-old live oak trees that stand like huge sculptures on the lawn; the resplendent peonies are bright notes in the middle of the sumptuous green expanses. The small bed of daffodils (their blooms gone by) with leaves neatly tied up in green twine make interesting shapes mixed together with the caladiums.

A raised bed by the pool house is an early summer shimmer of lupines, coralbells, columbines, irises, and gray-leaved lavender.

Beyond a flurry of columbines is the glass-domed Folly and adjacent greenhouses filled with orchids, exotic trees, and mammoth ferns.

A
BACKYARD
PARADISE

Banked up against The Red Crow antiques shop in Pound Ridge, New York, is a gloriously planted garden that extends down to a lazy pond and looks like a small and choice landscape painting with every detail rendered with immaculate care. It has the vitality of never-ending blooms, with dozens and dozens of specimen peonies from the Ozarks, masses of delphiniums, lupines, foxgloves, campanulas, and over twenty-seven different varieties of lilies.

Mulching, dead-heading, and harvesting flowers are the only garden chores, as there is almost no weeding to be done: the weeds don't have a chance to grow because of the dense planting. And *volunteers,* those plants that spring up out of the blue and seed themselves, are warmly welcomed. The summer spirit of come-one come-all is gracious, and the feeling is informal and friendly; for here, in this "careless order'd garden" the gate is always wide open.

In this song of summer the grace notes are brushstrokes of color, as the gardener here says, "there are no clashes in nature."

This wonderful garden gives one the desire to be Lilliputian and stand among these flowers dwarfed by the giant blooms. A favorite flower weaving through the mass is Malva sylvestris, a profuse blooming garden treasure that goes on all summer long, untroubled by insects or diseases.

An old cart serves as a planting bed for a display of sweet Williams and marigolds.

One perfect dahlia looms up proudly over just-planted white impatiens.

Classical sculptures are nestled among variegated Euonymus fortunei *'Silver Queen.'*

Gray dusty miller and white petunias border the brick paths.

Delphiniums, irises, and yellow evening primroses are spectacular down by the waterside; later there will be a sea of spiky cleomes blooming in pink and white clusters.

DESIGNED
FOR
SHADOWS

Landscape designer Maggie Daly, whose charming garden is pictured on the following pages, lectures on the subject of gardening; the following is her stream-of-thought advice on how to get the most rewarding use out of an intimate garden world.

Nan Fairbrother, an English landscape designer, wrote that we are trying to "convert to poetry the prose of the surrounding landscape." It is a lovely statement, and one to set you dreaming.

If you've lived in your house ten or fifteen years, no doubt it's time for a new slipcover, fresh wallpaper, a dramatic new color for your dining room, and what about the outdoors? Is the most important shrub by your front door leggy, never ever to return to the full lovely shape it once was? Take it out, perhaps it wasn't really needed there. Step back, take a good look at the whole area. Was that particular shrub doing anything for the front of your house? We live with what exists in our immediate surroundings without really seeing what is there. If you don't want professional help, ask your best gardening friend to come over and reappraise your property with you. Don't be *afraid* to ask. Cut down a big tree if it's in the center of your best view, on the other hand, plant a big tree if you've always wanted one in a certain spot. If your driveway lands everyone at the kitchen door and that bothers you, reroute your driveway if possible (if you can afford to).

If you're unhappy with the planting at the front of your house, take it all out and don't try to recycle the material unless some of it is in good condition. Redesign the shape of the beds, enlarge them, or lessen them. Use a hose for the line, play with it a lot until you are really satisfied, now consider scale, then material. Your material should be chosen for hardiness, texture and color. Don't use too many varieties, you'll create a jumpy effect. Don't use plants that are so small that dogs and children will step on them. Don't buy a two foot tree and wait ten years for it to make an effect. Labor will be your biggest cost—a bigger tree is not much more expensive. A ground cover planted at the base or a shrub border in a nice wide band will tie the planting together. Mix broad leaved evergreens and deciduous plants for the best effect. Some of the same principles for flower arrangements can be applied to planting. Odd numbers of a variety always seem to make the best effect, and fewer varieties with repetition of variety are important. Symmetrical planting creates formality, whereas asymmetrical does the opposite.

Study your property carefully, taking note of the best views, the sunny places and the shady ones, and where you have the most privacy. You can enhance an existing view (perhaps it needs just framing) or you can create a view by carving one out through your field of weeds. Paths winding through can intrigue—a series of endless lovely curves, with a surprise around each bend, in a bench, a piece of sculpture, a ground cover that is a splash of color. The surface of your path could be any material that suits: chips, gravel, or grass; and if you need a path from one place to another, don't make it until you see where the footsteps fall—animals make their paths using the gentlest grades. (But pay careful attention not to disturb a unique atmosphere, for preserving unity with existing nature is so important.) The lines and materials of your house should also be considered. Are you situated in a meadow? Then announce its beauty by playing it up. If you're in the woods, clear them enough to let natural light filter through the trees—the wild flowers will do better too.

Make a plan with everything in it you think you want and need. Discuss it, improve it, throw it away, start again. Your property will advise you, as will your family and your pocketbook. Decide how much you can do, do it in stages, don't allow yourself to become discouraged. Do one thing right away that will thrill you and make a big difference.

What do you and your family want your property to do for you to make your life more pleasant? Have you always wanted a picnic area away from the house so it's an adventure to go there? Consider all the qualities of your property, walk around it, sit in it, view it from indoors. What would you like and how much time can you give to these desires? If it's a vegetable garden, put it close to the kitchen, and make it a thing of beauty. People are always treating vegetable gardens as though they should be hidden. Mix flowers in with the plan and add a few dwarf fruit trees; position it so it can be seen in all its fruitful glory.

Any one of us with whatever piece of land we have can make it better. Cost comes into it, but more than the cost is the vision in your head and the determination in your heart to create that vision. If you've always wanted a pond where the spring is making a large damp spot, get it dug out, plant willows, build the bridge. On the other hand, take good stock of the overall picture. If there are dead trees and messy undergrowth that should be cleared, and your shrubs are up over your living room windows, and there is absolutely no definition to your driveway, then you should tend to these minor things first. You'll be amazed at the improvement. Don't underestimate the effectiveness of having good maintenance: replace stones on walks, pick up winter debris, prune, replace winter kill. There is no such thing as "no maintenance," and the more you do, the better everything will look. (There *are* ways to lessen maintenance: mulch your gardens heavily, consider different ground covers, and some mossy areas.)

Use colors that you love. I once had a white garden, but lovely as it was I *had* to have color. If there is a strong visual connection from your house to the garden, perhaps the garden should reflect your interior colors. My living room used to have a crimson wall. It is now deep pink, the entire room, and the garden which you look out at, needed to be changed from its oranges and yellows to relate to the pink interior. Hot colors make a space smaller, lavenders and blues fade away. Color will show up better against solids, stone walls, or an evergreen hedge.

Consider your winter landscape. Pick trees with good branching, so the winter silhouette will be good. Plant enough evergreens and berry bearing shrubs. Plant lots of early blooming bulbs to reassure yourself that spring is on the way. Consider the views

Over a bridge spanning a drainage ditch (not the "Pootatuck River" after all, as stated on the sign) a pine bark path winds lazily through the woods, over periwinkle and wild flowers showing in the spring. "Eighteen years ago you couldn't walk through the jungle; we've cleared and cleared so that now we have vistas with sparkles of light shining through the trees."

from all the important windows in your house. I love looking down on some of our garden from upstairs, especially in early spring.

I believe it is very important to everyone's spirit and peace of mind to be involved with nature, whether it be cutting a rose, picking your own spinach, or better still, walking around and enjoying your own territory—a creation of yourself hand-in-hand with nature.

Maggie Daly practices what she preaches and through the years she has tamed her own garden territory, carving out trees from woodland surrounding the house and letting the sun shine in to make dappled designs on her whole green scheme. The woods seem deeper, more magical and mysterious now, with shape and contrast and views that open up into glades and natural vistas, the paths strewn between wild flowers and ferns and periwinkle plateaus.

The planted garden beds border terraces with precise formality to form an outdoor living room and an outdoor dining room; the design works as an entertaining extension of the house, a bridge to the green country beyond. It is an elegant approach, an expressive way of meeting nature head-on, the formal and the informal: lines are drawn, but they merge, for each woodland tree and bush is as shaped and manicured as one of Mrs. Daly's sharply trimmed topiaries.

Here, nature is helped and improved on, and the planned planted garden of classical proportions becomes the leading star of the serendipitous wild woodland performance.

The terrace garden, enclosed with a curved brick wall, is circled with pink and red roses. Furnished with statues and carvings, a stone birdbath and big terra-cotta tubs of gardenias, the terrace becomes a stylish sitting room with trees for walls.

Houseplants summer over under the shade of an old swamp maple tree, and the surrounding ornamental beds, anchored with green mounds of boxwood, are filled with pink pelargoniums neatly edged with a miniature hedge of germander (Teucrium chamaedrys). The bees are quite partial to its profuse pink flowers.

Mrs. Daly's topiaries are decorative centerpieces, elegant and sculptural. The spirals are swirls of ivy and the circles are of ivy and the big-leaved Hoya carnosa 'Crimson Queen.'

The terrace just off the kitchen wing is an outdoor dining room; the table is set for a party with a hand-painted tablecloth and plates in fiesta colors.

A stone lion with a mane of ivy shares the dappled garden with pet rabbits.

A greyhound rests on a stone wall that marks the boundary of the field where an old-fashioned row-on-row vegetable garden produces prodigious amounts, including straw-berries and raspberries; the garlic, coming on strong, is a bee haven.

Celia Thaxter's favorite combination of oranges and yellows, with red poppies mixed in like burning torches. A bee has lighted on Centaurea macrocephala, a thistlelike bloom that comes on strong in June and July with stalks that sail about 48 inches high in the air.

ALL MAINE

The Thaxter Parlor as well as all the rooms of the summer cottage on Maine's Appledore Island were always ablaze with flowers, beautifully arranged every single day in a collection of over 100 different vases. The bountiful garden itself was admired by all who came to visit, and it was one of the most beloved and frequently painted gardens in America. Celia Thaxter (1835–1894), its originator, was a poet and essayist whose friends were luminaries of the era: Childe Hassam, Oliver Wendell Holmes, Candace Wheeler, John Greenleaf Whittier.

The Thaxter garden was especially inspirational to her friend of many years, the painter Childe Hassam, whose canvases of the island scene are as important to American impressionism as Monet's gardens at Giverny are to the French.

The cottage with all the exquisite flower arrangements is gone now (it burned in 1914), but the garden is kept up and is open to the public during the summer months.

In a way, all of Maine is one big picture-postcard garden, every bit as lovely as Celia Thaxter's famous one. The gardening there seems to be a way of life that complements the spectacular scenery—great gray boulders looming up everywhere and wind-sculpted pines as dark exclamations; a rugged coastline with the rolling mountaintops forms an undulating backdrop for sea and sky. Every blossom and leaf do appear to have a more brilliant hue than anywhere else: the air is purer, grass is greener, the ocean is bluer, and the flowers are more fragrant.

All the Maine gardens pictured here are a heady mix of color, texture, and scent, and the variety of plants and trees and ferns turns them into little paradises. What with all the rocky terrain, winds and salt spray, and the long stretches of fog and dampness (not to mention the deer), the gardens survive. James Dickinson of Maine's Surrey Gardens, a designer, a plantsman, and a lecturer, remarks on the very special quality of the gardens:

In looking through these pictures, imagine yourself standing in the center of each garden, in the middle of nature where the ferns and the native shrubbery and trees complement the cultivated flowers in such a way that one can scarcely say where the tame meets the wild—this wonderful blend is the secret of their charms.

A garden is nestled in the woods and naturalized in tiers with bark paths winding through its graceful tranquillity. The pale pink astilbe and ferns are outlined with snapdragons, petunias, and sweet alyssum. There are daisies, aconitums, hot pink phlox, delphinium, and later the beds will be brimming with purple, yellow, and white asters, pink lilies, and white cosmos. The seal sculptures, settled so happily on the rocks, are by Henry Mitchell.

Gardens are where you make them: Mrs. B's is on the edge of a cliff, and her flowers are as exhilarating as a fine day in Maine can be. When one sits in the garden, the edge seems to merge right into the water, and the harbor is framed with a sea of creamy astilbe, vibrant lilies, and pelargoniums.

The colors of the lilies are echoed in the shades of the umbrellas, like so many lollipops stuck in the grass.

A garden filled with summer magic is a great show of the silver grays and greens. In the corner in a cascade of foamy white is Macleaya microcarpa *(plume poppy). Lamb's ears are in the foreground edging and the other silvery-gray-leaved plants are artemisias.*

Some gardens have the perfect setting: neat stone walls to contain the flower borders and a panoramic view of the sea and the mountains. In the corner, just in front of the pink astilbe, is a clump of charming Iris setosa canadensis (I. hookeri), *which grows along the coast of Maine north to Labrador. Its seeds come from The Wild Gardens of Acadia in Bar Harbor, and being a dwarf variety, it can also make a suitable rock-garden plant.*

A cheerful garden is alive and happy with flittering butterflies and bees taking their fill of the lavender and bee balm plants. It is like an English cottage garden with a profusion of plants and beguiling scents; lilies, daylilies, and dianthus add their sweetness to the air. Since the house is contemporary, the gardener strived to make her garden nostalgic and old-fashioned for contrast.

Herbs and salad bowl lettuces are imaginatively mixed in with perennials in the half-moon bed that circles the terrace. Growing out of the stones are chamaecyparis (a slow-growing, matlike dwarf evergreen), a clump of yellow achillea, and varieties of dianthus plants, some smelling of cinnamon. The long border against the fence is filled with white phlox, white dwarf nicotiana, and daylilies, all prettily edged with fraises des bois. The dashes of orange are Lychnis chalcedonica, a bloomer that performs from May through August.

This garden on Little Cranberry Island goes back to the fall of 1954 when over fifty trees were felled after a hurricane. Once the land was cleared, modest flower borders were started, and over the years the dabs of color have turned into whole masses of rich displays basking in the sun. Neat stone enclosures contain the melee of painterly hues: the purples are tradescantia, the yellows are Oenothera fruticosa (common sundrops), and mixed in are splashes of white daisies, orange daylilies, and foxgloves, together with low-growing red astilbe and taller pink ones. The eighty-year-old gardener who lovingly tends it all counts these choice favorites as her best friends.

The hybrid mullein (verbascum) is a perfect treasure pictured against the lichen- and moss-covered fence.

The owner describes her garden as "a little bit of everything" kind of place, and she is as spirited as her enviable range of plants. Like a graphic patchwork quilt there are bold strokes of color that encompass a 30- by 70-foot plot enclosed by wire to protect it from the deer. To the rear are sunny clumps of coreopsis, red monarda, spires of Lythrum virgatum 'Morden Pink.' Just in front of the orange and yellow daylilies is astrantia, an easy-to-grow perennial with blush-pink blooms. To the left, vegetables take the spotlight with waves of asparagus, kale, collard greens, Swiss chard, lettuces, beans (and pea vines traveling up the wire netting), herbs, pink peonies, and yummy red nasturtiums. Nicotiana, phlox, asters, and even tuberoses share the plot. The paths between the patchwork plantings are lengths of straw matting.

The collarette dahlia is a wondrous combination of a frilled inner collar of yellow contrasting with the red outer petals.

Around a picturesque little tool house and a quiet pond, a hedge of ferns and beautifully pruned spruces turn a corner of a garden into contrasts of textures and shades of green.

A color and texture delight from the "little-bit-of-everything" garden: white phlox, red monarda, yellow lilies.

A soft path of sweet alyssum dotted with little campanulas sprawls over the rocks like a pointillist canvas. The tall, pale blue and white flowers to the left are monkshoods; the variety is Aconitum x bicolor, *which grows to about 48 inches high.*

THE HOWARD KNEEDLER GARDEN

Timeless and tranquil, this nurtured retreat was designed by the renowned Philadelphia landscape architect Howard Kneedler in 1956. The garden plan follows the tracks left by a forty-five-room, four-story summer cottage, a fortress on the shoreline that had burned to the ground. The old foundations are the bones for the new plantings; it is a pastoral delight as well as an adventure into the woods. The walks encompass over forty varieties of whispering trees and twenty different ferns, and they ramble over lichen and moss pine needles. The adventure is like moving through a series of outdoor rooms filled with sculptures and surprises, each one leading to the next and all flowing together in a natural way.

The land, planted with native evergreens, dwarf conifers, and ferns, sweeps down in grassy paths between stones of the old foundations. At the extreme right, a sculpture from Kyoto is tucked into a flamboyant spray of Japanese irises.

Flower beds are muted pastel scenes of pink astilbe, white campanula, yellow dahlias, pansies, and snapdragons. Lobelia, alternating with vanilla-scented white and purple heliotrope, threads around the contours; and gray artemisias are silvery clouds that hover between the plantings. Beyond this, the walks wander through a woodland garden of one-and-three-quarter acres of fascinating trees and ferns, mosses and sculptures.

Mossy stepping-stones lead to a surprise clearing among the pitch pines where old quarrystones stand strong as sculptures of age and permanence.

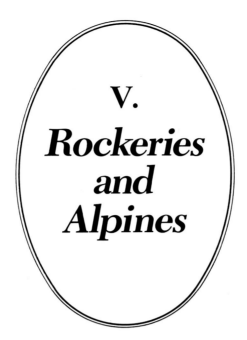

V.
Rockeries and Alpines

SMALL JEWELS
FROM
AROUND THE WORLD

I like my flowers small and delicate—the taste of all gardeners, as their discrimination increases, dwindles towards the microscopic.

Vita Sackville-West, *A Joy of Gardening*

The enchanting thing about alpines is they are so very small and so very spectacular. In their native habitats they are delicate-looking little beauties that sprout glorious colors in the most outlandish places, and true alpine aficionados will track them down, hiking great distances up steep tracks to exotic rocky slopes even to such remote places as Rungdum Gömpa in Tibet. Alpines thrive in the grit and gravel, the bogs and screes and meadows above the treeline on mountaintops. Incredibly tenacious, there are a few kinds that will grow only in one very limited area in the whole wide world; such as pink *Primula duclouxii* that gets a roothold in the limestone cliffs (2,250 miles above sea level) near Long Men in the West Hills of Kunming, Yünnan.

The smallest of all the forget-me-nots, *Anchusa caespitosa*, is found only on the summit of Mount Olympus in Greece. Kabschia saxifrages are from the higher reaches of the European Alps, and the dwarf cyclamen comes from the mountains of Lebanon and Turkey. The Lewisias come from our own western mountains and are named after Meriwether Lewis of Lewis and Clark, who first discovered them on their expedition (1803–1806) across the country to explore the territory of the Louisiana Purchase. The *Primula* species (there are over 400 of them) come from the Caucasus, the Altai Mountains, the

Himalayas, the Maritime Alps of France, and other temperate regions, chiefly of the Northern Hemisphere. Their history in cultivation dates back more than 500 years:

Of all alpines most precious and easy and hardy is *Primula auricula,* with its huge mealy leaves, lying out upon the grey rock like fat hoary star-fishes; and its stalwart heads of blossom are of the imperial Chinese yellow.... All the forms of *P. auricula* are of the easiest culture anywhere in the rock garden, to such a degree, indeed, that its children and grandchildren have become ordinary border plants. For *P. auricula* freely breeds with other species that share its alps.... All the offspring have to be lumped under the one name of *P. x pubescens,* and to *P. pubescens* belongs the whole vast race of garden auriculas, being descendants, inbred and interbred through ages, of the original crosses, *P. auricula* with *P. viscosa, P. hirsuta,* and *P. villosa.* These hybrids are fertile too, and breed again in and out with each other endlessly and then back again to their parents; so that there is no real differentiating them, or distinguishing them by any but fancy names such as 'The General,' or 'Mrs. J. H. Wilson.' These hybrids, with their children, have been in cultivation at least since the sixteenth century, when Clusius saw them in the garden of his friend Dr. Aicholtz of Vienna about 1560, and vainly sought them accordingly in the Austrian and Styrian ranges.

Reginald Farrer, *The English Rock-Garden*

Hikers taking a wild flower holiday in the Alps of Switzerland, Austria, or Germany in June and July are apt to see in bloom the yellow *Primula auricula*, the rosy-pink *Primula hirsuta*, the delicate pink *Primula farinosa* with daisylike eyes, and the pale yellow *Primula elatior*. Meadows with carpets of these little blooms are breathtaking, and to have them down from 7,000 feet in a sunny spot in a rock garden is also breathtaking. They do just fine.

The late Reginald Farrer, a plant collector and gardener as well as a writer, is credited with developing the techniques for helping alpines to thrive in ordinary gardens: he planted his specimens in mountain-growing conditions with plenty of drainage. The trick was (and it still applies today) to put crushed rock under the plants and to blend gravel into the soil mix. Then after planting with a dash of bonemeal, another layer of gravel or chipped stone is added to help keep the moisture in. Cool tops, dry feet seems to be the theory. (Some alpines prefer shade over sun, some like an acidic rather than a lime soil, some grow in bogs.) The bible for gardeners is H. Lincoln and Laura Foster's book, *Rock Gardening* (Beaverton, Oreg.: Timber Press, 1982), which tells all. In their famous Connecticut garden, Millstream, they have six acres of rock gardens filled with plants garnered from all over the world, tucked around in bogs, screes, moraines, and rocky outcroppings of the land, all looking perfectly natural.

Gathering seeds from all over the world is part of the fun of growing alpines. Wonderfully romantic trips can be envisioned while reading advertisements for searching out alpines on flower holidays:

SOME 1983 SPRING FLOWER HOLIDAYS
ST. LUC—THE VAL D'ANNIVIERS
30 JUNE TO 12 JULY WITH DR. MARTYN RIX M.A., Ph.D., F.L.S.

This charming little village at over 5000 ft. is sunny and south-facing with magnificent views of the Valaisan Alps, including the Besso, the Zinal Rothorn, the Dent Blanche and the north face of the Matterhorn. There are walks of all kinds, long and short, and plenty of excursions can be made into the other parts of the valley. It is famous for the wealth and variety of its alpine flora and is still one of the really unspoiled places in Switzerland. 13 days: £415.

Or this offer to go to unpronounceable places to stalk the wild flowers and to be introduced to the culture of the country.

PLAN DE GRALBA—THE DOLOMITES
9 TO 21 JULY WITH MR. DAVID PATON M.A., F.L.S., A.R.P.S.

At 6168 ft. this is the highest village in the Val Gardena and about two miles from Seiva, the nearest place of any size in the vicinity. Botanically there is much of interest as it is in a Dolomitic limestone region, moreover it is within walking distance of the Rodella ridge of volcanic origin, with a complete change of flora. This tour is of special interest to keen walkers. There are, however, chairlifts in the vicinity and excursions can be arranged locally to the Gardena Pass and over to Corvara and Colfosco, as well as to many other places of enormous interest. 3 days: £419.

UZBEKHISTAN—CENTRAL ASIA
24 APRIL TO 8 MAY WITH DR. MARTYN RIX M.A., PH.D., F.L.S.

The emphasis on this tour is given to exploring the most botanically exciting area reached from Samarkand, Bokhara, Tashkent and Fergana while still allowing time for sightseeing in these historic and beautiful cities. The last day is spent in Leningrad. 15 days: £940.

THE CAUCASUS—OSSETIA, GEORGIA AND RUSSIAN ARMENIA
10 TO 26 JUNE WITH MR. OLEG POLUNIN M.A., F.L.S.

This journey into the high mountains, from Ordzhonikdize along the Georgian Military Highway to Kasbegi and thence by way of Tbilisi to Erevan, is dramatic indeed and a rare experience for both the ardent traveller and the botanist. Enough time is spent at each one of the three main centres to appreciate the profusion and variety of the local flora and, at Tbilisi, a day in which to visit some of the fine museums and art galleries for which it is famous. 17 days: £950.

And equally unromantic can be frank accounts of such adventures:

"How do you manage to retain your health and stamina on these long mountain trips?", is a question often asked. Here, then, follows a simple but incomplete guide, from the pen of one youthful Yorkshireman who visited the Hautes Alpes, Maritimes and Dolomites last year, to ensure physical and mental equilibrium in these exacting conditions.

06.30 hours... crawl out of sleeping bag, remove jeans and shirt, give them a good shake and replace immediately before everything human and material freezes. Stroll to nearest water source to perform rudimentary ablutions, then return to tents making loud noises indicating one is ready for breakfast... Muesli, bread and apricot jam. Anything left over from supper will be eaten by the gannet. Every expedition has one of these scavengers.

In due course the day's search begins, but first there must be orientation exercises. Getting lost seems integral to the discovery of *Ranunculus glacialis* or *Campanula morettiana*. A compass is useful if it is cloudy, as also would be an Ordnance Survey map, Michelin is a last resort. Our friend says he likes to allow a little extra time for this exercise to be able to rove with eye and mind across frontiers, pinnacles and along vast ridges all sitting on top of or in the clouds....I know the feeling when the only visible fixed point for a bearing is the drip on the end of one's nose. There is no shortage of general exercise in the Alps, an interesting variation is scree walking. 3000 feet upwards an hour should show how fit you are. At Monte Cristallo the route is well marked by the overhead cable car so getting lost is unlikely. The bombardment by loose boulders is quite terrifying and dangerous. This form of Russian roulette is not recommended for the faint hearted.

As for food and drink the variety is splendid, local fruit can be as fresh as the local brew, but do not expect to locate *Saxifraga florulenta* on Grade 5 faces after imbibing, and even if totally temperate remember only the highest streams are likely to be safe unboiled these days. So it goes on, but it's a great life if you don't weaken. (*Bulletin* of the Alpine Garden Society of England)

The American Rock Garden Society is fifty years old this year. Headquarters are in Asheville, North Carolina, appropriately near the Carolina Smokies, one of our richest areas for endemic American plants, and home base for all kinds of lovely flowers like terrestrial orchids, trillium species, galax, trailing arbutus, and hosts of others. Every year the society sends out a list of seeds of almost 5,000 different plants contributed by people from all over the world. Of immense scope and variety, this mammoth list is largely owing to men like Henry Correvon, who wrote this lament long ago:

When, fifty years ago, I spoke here in Geneva of the culture of alpine plants and of rock gardening, I was considered a foolish man, and people were sorry for me. I remember that, in 1877, being a young man and wishing to extend the culture of mountain plants, I ventured to make an exhibit of alpine plants grown from seeds before the Société d'Horticulture de Genève at a spring show. The judges and the Committee were surprised, and hesitated to accept mountain flowers in an exhibition of garden plants. They considered these wild plants as weeds; as one of them jocularly said: *Jardin alpin—herbe à lapins.* The judges were perplexed to know how to treat the small collection, and thought it was not worth acknowledgement; but one of them said: "Give him something in order to prove the interest which the Society shows in encouraging young beginners," and they gave me four little silver spoons!

Rock Garden and Alpine Plants

The millions of porcelainlike little plants gathered through the years is a glorious and vast mixed bounty of wild and cultivated ones—and one of the nicest surprises is that gardening with these miniatures can be quite easy. They can create clouds on top of rocks (the white iberis) or canopies on terraces (*Liriope spicata*) or patchwork spots of color for stone walls and stairs. The moss pinks, dianthus, sedums, and woolly thyme plants need virtually no care at all and can be tucked into the smallest places between stonework. At the base of a rock garden a little Alpine meadow could flourish: fuzzy lamb's ears (*Stachys byzantina*) would make a silver ribbon to weave through blue auriculas, there could be scented plants, such as primula and leontopodium (edelweiss), pink *Daphne cneorum eximia*, white *Petrocallis pyrenaica*, yellow *Coronilla valentina*, all tolerant of adverse conditions and all low-maintenance. There are others, suggested by the American Rock Garden Society:

Achillea ageratifolia	*Coreopsis auriculata*
A. tomentosa	'Nana'
Alchemilla alpina	*Dianthus* 'Tiny Rubies'
Androsace sarmentosa	and others
Anemone pulsatilla	*Draba aizoides*
Aquilegia discolor	*D. olympica*
A. flabellata 'Nana'	*Epimedium*, several
Arabis caucasica	kinds
Arenaria montana	*Gentiana scabra*
Armeria juniperifolia	*Geranium cinereum*
A. maritima	*G. sanguineum*
Astilbe chinensis 'Pumila'	prostratum
Campanula carpatica	*Globularia cordifolia*
C. elatines garganica	*Gypsophila repens*
C. portenschlagiana	*Hosta venusta*
Chrysogonum	*Iberis*, several kinds
virginianum	*Iris crisata*

I. graminea	*S. middendorffianum*
Lychnis alpina	*Sempervivum*, several
Penstemon hirsutus	kinds
'Pygmaeus'	*Solidago spathulata*
Potentilla tabernaemon-	'Nana'
tani (P. verna 'Nana')	*Thalictrum kiusianum*
Saponaria ocymoides	*Thymus*, several kinds
Sedum dasyphyllum	*Veronica*, several kinds

These perennial plants, whether alpine or otherwise, all share an affinity for small spaces. They can be grown anywhere, in crevices, in troughs, in shallow sinks. A rock garden, with its hill and dale and plateau areas, supplies the perfect place to plant all the alpines and diminutives; rock walls, with good drainage and cool rooting spots, make ideal havens for plants that would die elsewhere: *Alyssum saxatile* and its variety *A. saxatile citrinum; Corydalis lutea;* aubrieta; arabis; *Phlox subulata;* alpine strawberry, and alpine clematis are all gems that take to rock enclosures and become lovelier year after year.

The joy of the smalls is not only in growing some of the world's rarest plants from faraway places but in situating them in suitable and appropriate places...a gardener works closely within nature to create this alliance of native habitat and new home.

Photograph by Ted Hardin

THE GARDEN AT UPLANDS

Neptune, flanked with a white dogwood and a Japanese red maple, dominates a small pool, in harmony with the ground-hugging creeping thymes clamoring over the rocks. The troughs hold sedums, rock plants that embody the incredible global range of small and rare specimens that grow throughout the garden. It is a spectacular panorama, a kaleidoscope of seasonal tufts and mounds of fragile-looking miniatures. They all seem to be in partnership with nature, happily wedded to their rocky cliff homes.

Highlights at the base of a tree, starting at the top of the colorful spill: the little purple bells are Symphyandra wanneri *(a biennial); the pink, peppermint-striped flowers are* Lewisia cotyledon *(one of the plants discovered by Meriwether Lewis of the Lewis and Clark expedition); the fragile-looking little yellow posies to the far right (with the columbine-type leaves) are* Corydalis lutea; *and the spread of yellow stars in the foreground is* Chrysogonum virginianum.

The glints of pink popping up out of the rocks are Dianthus alpinus
*'Millstream' ("Millstream" in a plant name means it was propagated by
the country's leading rock gardener and speaker and author on the
subject, H. Lincoln Foster, whose garden at his home, Millstream,
is such a mecca for plant enthusiasts).*

*A natural, seemingly effortless effect of rock formation woven like a crocketwork of color, sunshine on
stone, with* Papaver alpinum *being the main plant in bloom. This is a bed made up of sand, leaf mold,
gravel, peat, and tufa stone (tufa is a natural formation made from the deposits of minerals in much
the same way that stalactites and stalagmites are formed).*

Papaver alpinum *is the main plant in bloom.*

This showstopper is lady's slipper, the native representative of the orchid family:
Cypripedium calceolus parviflorum.

A granite wall cascades with color, a paint box of plants running together on the raised bed above it and peeking out through the crevices. The deep purple curve is fashioned of Veronica prostrata 'Rosea'; its pink tip is Dianthus 'La Bourbrille.' The rock formation itself imitates scree, which is the loose gravel often found at the base of mountain slopes.

This little pink-flowered plant, which seems to have seeded itself in another spot on the rock, is Penstemon rupicola.

THE PARROT
GARDEN

A tall outcropping of high rock wears a mantle of color, its tumbling palette of blooms flourishing in an artless, more natural way. The transformation is a hillscape of dianthus, phlox, saponaria, armeria, chrysogonum, and cytisus, all carpetlike plantings that lead from one level to another over weathered rocks. Even though the up, up, and on up scene looks like a mountainous vista that rises for miles, it is really a two-story boulder that rises smack up against the side of a house, a miniature hill where one can see eye-to-eye the immediate delicacy of the flowers. But looking up is like ascending a mountainside, a trip around the world.

Botanically, there *is* peaceful coexistence between countries, and gardeners exchange seeds freely. A lot of the flowers that make up this garden came from seeds supplied by a good friend in Czechoslovakia.

From the Pyrenees comes a relative of the African violet: Ramonda myconi.

This jewel makes a bright show against the brown pine needles: Saponaria ocymoides 'Rubra compacta.'

The glowing range of plant life perched in the nooks and crannies begins with Linaria supina, *the white spiky plant in front of the conifer; then saponarias in two shades of pink; and a light pink dianthus from Czechoslovakia.*

The dazzling white Cerastium tomentosum *(snow-in-summer) spreads rapidly over New England's gray, lichened rocks and grows like a weed.*

Hedyotis (Houstonia) caerulea, *called Quaker-ladies or bluets, is common along the roadsides. In front of it is a very healthy weed.*

The gardener's comment on the linaria: "This is a hybrid that appeared spontaneously in my garden, in another location, and I propagated it from cuttings and tried it in various places—here in this narrow crack in the rock, it has been most long-lived."

THE
CABOT COLLECTION

Here are entrancing specimens from Frank Cabot's collection of starlike saxifrages at Stonecrop. The Saxifragaceae comprise an enormous family of plants (there are about 300 species); one could fill a large rock garden with them and still not be able to grow all the varieties. There are three main classes: encrusted (or silver, because the leaves are covered with silvery deposits), kabschia, and mossy. Most of the encrusted are easy to grow; the kabschia are sometimes difficult; and the mossy ones are very easy. These diminutive alpine "rock-breakers" can grow up through crevices, as their roots like to burrow into rocky hillsides.

Besides saxifrages, there are hundreds of varieties of alpines and rock plants to order from Stonecrop, Cold Spring, New York 10516; Cable: Saxifrage.

Photograph by Ted Hardin

Photograph by Ted Hardin

P.S.: GARDEN BLIGHTS
by Barbara Cheney

The following postscript is reprinted from old Maine garden club notes as an insight into one gardener's feelings after showing off her own carefully tended garden to friends.

Gardening, I told myself, is the most sociable of hobbies. The very nature of one's field of activities demands an audience. No one wants flowers to blush unseen or waste their sweetness. This was what I thought until last week.

Last week I worked hard, weeding, setting out new plants, dividing old ones. When at last I arose from my muddy knees, I felt elated, though weary, and eager to display the fruits of my labors. My first hope was an old friend who dropped in for tea. I restrained my impatience until she had been properly fed. Then I led her forth.

"Oh yes," she cried, "I'd love to see your garden. I'm so fond of flowers."

As we neared the scene of my triumphs, and I was slowing down to begin my introductory speech, she tucked her arm in mine and said, "I'm so glad to have a chance to chat with you alone. We have so many, many weeks to catch up."

"Yes, indeed," I said vaguely. "Now here is the entrance, you see. I'm very proud of my iris. I planned these clumps myself so that I have three months of continuous bloom."

"How nice," she said. "Have you heard from Ann lately?"

"No" I said, thinking to block that detour. It was the wrong answer.

"Well, I have," said my guest, firmly planting her foot on my favorite sedum. "She's been to a psychoanalyst and has a new ego—not a very nice one, if you ask me." Nothing would have induced me to ask her, but that made no difference. I learned all about Ann's ego.

"We'll stay here by these clumps of iris until she looks at them," I thought, but I finally took pity on the sedum and led her on. Ann's ego absorbed her until we had passed the peonies, about which I was bursting to talk. At last she paused for breath.

"You must notice my Scotch broom," I said hastily. "It's very rare in this country."

"Did you know the Scotts were getting a divorce?" she asked. This time I knew better than to say no.

"Yes," I said, concealing my surprise, "I heard all about it." But that didn't work, either.

"Oh, did you?" she said. "I doubt if you know the whole truth. Few people do." The whole truth carried us past my violas, my prize lupines, my rare old pinks. The only interruption was when she fell over the watering pot.

"I didn't see it," she explained.

"No," I said coldly, "you weren't looking."

It was several days before I recovered from this interview. I chose my next visitor more carefully. She was a real gardener, deeply interested in gardens, and she approached mine as eagerly as I did.

"The hedge," I explained, "has not recovered from the terrible winter of 1962. It died right down to the ground."

"Don't talk to me about the winter of '62," she cried.

"Do you know that I lost two box bushes that were a hundred years old, and that lovely 'Dr. Van Fleet' rose that I planted myself in 1940?"

I expressed genuine sympathy and then began again. "I'm very proud of my iris," I said.

"Have you any 'Ambassadeur's'?" she asked. "You must get some. Mine are beautiful. They actually stand almost three feet high. I have another new variety, too—'Moonlight.' It's perfectly beautiful."

I hurried her on to the peonies. "These I divided and set out myself," I said proudly, knowing that a real gardener would appreciate what a feat this was.

"You have no single ones, have you?" she asked. "I have the prettiest ones, pale pink, the Japanese variety. You must come over and look at them before they go by."

I was speechless after this, but she was not. My lovely blue lupines reminded her of her lovelier pink ones, my violas of the apricot ones she had at last achieved.

"Haven't you any dahlias?" she asked.

"No," I said firmly, "I hate them."

"Oh, but my dear, you wouldn't hate mine if you once saw them. The flowers are five inches across, they really are, and such lovely colors. I have some extra roots. I'll send them over."

"What I really want," I said to myself plaintively, "is someone who will look at my garden and think about my garden for just a few minutes. It doesn't seem too much to ask." It wasn't. I found her. She was the worst of all.

"I'm very proud of my iris," I began.

"My dear," she cried, "how beautiful they are! I never saw a prettier combination of colors. Those pale lavender ones next to the deep purple are perfect, and that touch of yellow adds just the right contrast." My soul began to expand.

"They are so perfect," she went on, "I think they ought to be where they would show off more. Couldn't you put them over there with the stone wall for a background?"

"The peonies are there now," I protested. "I set those all out myself. You have no idea what a job it was digging up the old roots and dividing them."

"Well, if I were you," she said, "I'd put the peonies over here."

"Yes," I said doubtfully, "but these lupines took five years to grow, and they don't move well once they're established."

"Oh, my dear," she said, "that's what the books tell you, but don't you believe it. You can move anything if you do it carefully. Speaking of moving," she went on, "I'm not sure I wouldn't move that hedge. It seems to me it would be more effective if you set it back about three feet."

"Next year," I said, "I'm going to have a new hedge, a very tall one, made entirely of thorns."

BIBLIOGRAPHY

Gertrude Jekyll was the garden writer who revolutionized English garden perceptions over ninety years ago, and her books on color, texture, and form are still remarkable reading today. *The Making of a Garden, Gertrude Jekyll,* an anthology compiled by Cherry Lewis, is a lively sampling of Miss Jekyll's vivid ideas that can be copied today. Her best-known contribution to turn-of-the-century English gardening was the herbaceous border. She orchestrated colors and considered white to be the color of light, which made everything beautiful: to her, the most pleasing blend for a border was a given color combined with a lighter shade of the same color, all illuminated with white.

Another famous gardener, the English poet and novelist Vita Sackville-West, originated (along with her husband Harold Nicolson) Sissinghurst Gardens, an enduring and triumphant creative achievement. Sissinghurst was opened to the public in 1938, and it is the most famous garden in the world. *Sissinghurst,* by Anne Scott-James, is the story of style and lavish design in the planning and planting of these unique gardens. Vita Sackville-West believed in thick planting in bold profusion: she liked plants tumbling together, with interplanting and underplanting and plants intertwining. Exaggeration, in big groups and big masses, was her style. During her lifetime she wrote prolifically about gardens and was widely celebrated as a gardening VIP. She won many horticultural honors, and one can only guess at her reaction to a famous instance of her mother's artful style of gardening. The story is that Lady Sackville-West invited her daughter to luncheon one day, and suddenly realized that there was nothing blooming in her garden that could possibly impress her daughter. She quickly sent out for fake blooms—velvet flowers, wax flowers, even beaded and sequined flowers—and stuck them all around her garden. We have no record of Vita Sackville-West's reaction to this display.

Fifty years ago Beverley Nichols wrote about his gardens the way that M. F. K. Fisher writes today about food—in a most intimate and personal way—a way that tells as much about the architecture of gardening as it does about the heart and soul of the art. Nichols's witty books are filled with tales of garden-growing traumas interlaced with village dramas. His best-known book, *Down the Garden Path,* is bountiful with garden lore, with sound advice, and with delightful aphorisms, to wit: "A garden is the only mistress who never fades, who never fails."

Following is detailed information about the aforementioned books and others that will reward your reading and study:

Beckett, Kenneth A., and Stevens, David. *The Contained Garden: A Complete Illustrated Guide to Growing Plants, Flowers, Fruits, and Vegetables Outdoors in Pots.* New York: The Viking Press, 1983.

Ferguson, Nicola. *Right Plant, Right Place: The Indispensable Guide to the Successful Garden.* New York: Summit Books, 1984.

Genders, Roy. *The Cottage Garden and the Old Fashioned Flowers.* Topsfield, Mass.: Merrimack Pubs. Circle, 1983.

Johnson, Hugh. *The Principles of Gardening.* New York: Simon & Schuster, 1984.

Lewis, Cherry, ed. *The Making of a Garden, Gertrude Jekyll.* Woodbridge, Suffolk (England): The Antique Collectors' Club, 1984.

Lloyd, Christopher. *The Well-Chosen Garden.* New York: Harper & Row, 1984.

Nichols, Beverley. *Down the Garden Path.* Norwood, Pa.: Norwood Editions, 1978.

Perenyi, Eleanor. *Green Thoughts: A Writer in the Garden.* New York: Random House, 1981.

Scott-James, Anne. *Sissinghurst: The Making of a Garden.* Topsfield, Mass.: Merrimack Pubs. Circle, 1984.

Verey, Rosemary. *Classic Garden Design.* New York: Congdon & Weed, 1984.

——. *The Scented Garden.* New York: Van Nostrand Reinhold, 1981.

For basic instruction, The Brooklyn Botanic Garden publishes good, informative booklets. They have about ninety-six in print and all are excellent. The cost is around $2.50 each. To receive a brochure of their illustrated publications, write to their headquarters at 1000 Washington Avenue, Brooklyn, New York 11225. Also, some of the most enjoyable booklets for both real and armchair gardeners are the color-illustrated catalogues issued by White Flower Farm, Litchfield, Connecticut 06759, and by Wayside Gardens, Hodges, South Carolina 29695.

PATRICIA CORBIN is a former *New York Times* reporter who has worked as a special projects editor for both *House & Garden* and *House Beautiful.* Her previous books are: *All About Wicker* (1978), *Designers Design for Themselves* (1980), and *Summer Cottages and Castles* (1983), all published by E. P. Dutton.

SOUTHIE BURGIN was a photographer of children for ten years, and currently she is a free-lance photographer in New York City specializing in interior design.

Photograph by Schecter Lee